HOME BOOZE

HOME BOOZE

*A complete guide
for the amateur wine-
and beer-maker*

H.E. Bravery

*Illustrations by
Jon Rogers*

BOOK CLUB ASSOCIATES LONDON

Printed in Great Britain by
St Edmundsbury Press, Bury St Edmunds, Suffolk

CONTENTS

(v)

Contents

Home Booze

Author's Note

This book gives you the widest possible range of ultra-modern, tried and tested recipes and fool-proof methods for making every type and variety of wine. The beer-making section is equally comprehensive.

The real value of the book is that it contains the best parts of three of my world-wide bestsellers, plus thirty-five years of practical experience in evolving hundreds of recipes and methods that have been accepted as the most reliable throughout the world. I did not set out to achieve this, as you will read in later pages. I merely set out all those years ago to find out why wines made in the home were so poor, and outright failures ninety times out of a hundred. The fact that my recipes and methods took the home wine-making world by storm is purely incidental. No one could have been more surprised than I when they won world acclaim and my books sold virtually by the million. But do not imagine that this Bumper Book is a rehash of earlier works. It is the best of my earlier works completely modernized in the light of progress in wine- and beer-making. It also contains a wealth of new recipes and methods for making wines which can be drunk in a few weeks, as well as those which – as we all know – take a few months to reach their best. So we have the 'quicky wines' to use almost right away while we are making the better-class wines that need time to develop their full strength, bouquet, body and quality.

Naturally a book of this sort must contain technical information, but this does not make wine- and beer-making difficult. Indeed, it makes it easier. The simple fact is that after reading about the causes of spoilage you may start off to make top-class wines. The information is there for you to digest at your leisure and use as background knowledge. Wine- and beer-making is like driving a car. You will be a much better driver if you know how the engine works and how the various parts rely upon each other for satisfactory performance; such a driver will know at once if some small part of the engine is not working properly. And

(1)

so it is with wine- and beer-making. When you have digested the technical information contained in this book you will be like that driver; you will know if something is not working out according to plan and be able to rectify matters accordingly. Now what could be better than that?

H.E. Bravery
April 1976

Part 1
WINE-MAKING

INTRODUCTION

This is not intended to be a history of amateur wine-making. However as a wine-maker of over thirty-five years' practical experience, with a number of years in beer-making (though I ought not to mention this because until April 1963 I was breaking the law), I do feel that wine-makers of today who enjoy using simple reliable methods and recipes should know something of the work that has been necessary in their evolution.

Thirty-five years ago home-made wines were poor indeed compared with those made today. Modern methods are the results of work by questing thinkers who were not satisfied as our forebears were to shrug off a failure as just one of those things.

My grandparents made vast amounts of wines, beers and ciders. My parents did likewise. Both became famous in their localities for the beverages they made. Some were good according to the tastes, standards and requirements of the average wine-drinker of the times, but none of them would be able to stand on their own feet today, any more than a local who had taken more than two pints of grandfather's beer or cider.

Despite the reputation they enjoyed, like countless others up and down the country, they had their failures. Naturally, they never told of them. The fact that they made so many good lots is remarkable when one considers, in the light of our present-day knowledge of the subject, that they were using the very methods that brought failures more often than success.

The normal practice was to gather the fruit and crush it, add water and sugar without boiling either and, without adding yeast, merely let it ferment by any yeast that was on the fruits or floating about in the air. Flowers were treated in the same fashion. No wonder they had so many failures. By failures I do not mean those over-acid, often insipid, muddy-looking concoctions accepted as wines by those who knew no better. These were merely disappointing lots to be used up when no one was around to see them, the better being kept for when someone worth impressing turned up, which was often.

I can recall vividly those great tubs containing forty gallons and more of wines and beers, their foaming heads alive with wasps and flies crawling all over them. No one thought of covering the vessels to guard against dust from beaten carpets and sifted ashes. Everything blew through the winery. And the converted pigsty in which my grandfather, and later my father, brewed their famed beers, was equally unhygienic. This state of affairs was common place. When I often had to run errands for the 'gentry' living in the 'big houses' in the area (not having been born with a silver spoon in my mouth) I used to see wines and beers being made under similar conditions, any barn or outhouse being suitable.

At eight or nine years old all I knew of wines and beers was that they made some people sing and others fight. But wines were made long before this. They were made before Noah – that is if you can believe that story of the Ark without having taken a drink or two first. Indeed, they were made by the most primitive of men. One reads in accounts by early explorers of concoctions made by natives chewing herbs, nuts or other materials and spitting the 'cud' into a vessel which later became the fermentation vessel. All members of the tribe are said to have taken turns at chewing and spitting until the vessel contained sufficient material. It was then fermented by whatever yeast happened to come along.

Explorers and early travellers spoke highly of the concoctions turned out in this fashion, probably before they had seen how they were made. One often reads of the wine-like drinks turned out by such and such tribe, 'a delightful beverage which when indulged in makes one merry'. I imagine many of the so-called 'love potions' were little more than crude alcohol produced in similar fashion. After all, most of us are a little less inhibited when we have had a drink or two. Dusky maidens knowing this tempted shy young warriors with a half coconut shell of this stuff and most likely took a little themselves to help things along. It was then easy to persuade the young bloods to make love. Thus this special love-potion was nothing more than a drop of spittoon wine. Personally, having seen some really lovely dusky maidens, I am at a loss to understand the need for love potions!

These wines, if you can call them that, are still being made today. And, as my considerable mail proves, people in this country, Canada, USA, Australia, New Zealand and the world over are still, alas, following the antiquated methods used by my grandparents. This is understandable up to a point because these were the methods taken to these countries by the pioneers, and so there are still thousands not yet acquainted with the few scientific details and scraps of equipment needed to transform their wines into something worth having.

Naturally, my early efforts were made by the same old methods. But I was not content. There must be a reason for all the disappointments and failures, I told myself, otherwise how could the trade turn out such wonderful stuff.

The trade was unlikely to give much help to those striving to find the secrets. There were no books on the subject other than collections of recipes following the methods already described. Even the immortal Mrs Beeton who was supposed to know everything could not give a clue. Not being a chemist and not realizing that there might be a chemical aspect to the subject, I continued making wines in this antiquated fashion always trying to find out the reason for those nagging faults – vinegariness, over-acidity, cloudiness and all the rest – that were to mar almost all our efforts.

Encyclopaedias were studied for hours, days, even weeks. Clues and possibilities were considered. But I and those helping me still felt we were battering our heads against a wall.

And then, quite by chance, we discovered some useful information about yeasts, the various sorts, their uses and effects. First we learned that some yeasts were suitable for making wines, while others floating about in the air were capable of ruining them. At last we were to understand that most of the disappointments and failures were due to 'unwanted' or 'undesirable' yeasts, and that these were on the very fruits we were making wines with. This was a great thrill indeed. For here was the root cause of disaster – contained in the very ingredients. (See Chapter 3 'Spoilage'.)

Boil to destroy was the obvious answer and we worked accordingly, destroying the yeast on the fruits and adding fresh yeast when the must had cooled. But our wines, while better in flavour and body, were almost always very cloudy. Popular clarifiers like isinglass and gelatine only worsened matters.

Some cleared to brilliance without the use of clarifiers. This deepened the mystery; why should some clear in this fashion and other refuse to clear even when 'clarified' with clarifiers? After a long time we learned something about pectin and how this is boiled into fruit juices, preventing wines from clearing. But we had to boil to destroy unwanted yeast, didn't we? It seemed at this stage that there was no method for making clear wines.

We continued to experiment, learning as we went along more about yeasts and bacteria, and we discovered how to destroy the unwanted yeasts and the bacteria on fruits without boiling them. The result was brilliantly clear wines with a better flavour, more body and bouquet. The wonderful stuff that made all this possible is known as sodium metabisulphite and is now available in tablet form as Campden fruit-preserving tablets.

That we had discovered nothing new to the science of wine-making did not dishearten us. For we were, I am sure, the first group of people to employ this chemical in wine-making, outside the trade. Thus we are able to take credit for introducing this type of wine-making to the world.

But I still had no real answer to another problem. Good wines that cleared to brilliance, had top-rate flavour, excellent bouquet and fair alcohol content were now easy to make, but they often spoilt on keeping. Yeast and bacteria are in the air, and must therefore be inside the very bottles we fill and on the corks we use to close them. So we had not only to sterilize bottles and corks, but also to keep air away during all stages of production, for the very air we breathe is death to our wines. Campden solution sterilized bottles; corks had to be boiled whether it harmed them or not. Today we have plastic corks which last a lifetime and are sterilized with Campden solution.

And so we were another stage nearer complete success. The final link in this mysterious chain came with the introduction of what I have often described as the best friend wine-makers will ever have – the fermentation lock. This little bit of twisted glass tubing forms the mighty 'wall of China' behind which our wines are safe from attack from outside.

Not only does this prevent spoilage yeasts and bacteria reaching the wines, but it assists in increasing the alcohol content which means that wines are preserved by the amount of alcohol present. And so we had, after many, many years of work, discovered secrets withheld from us; I say this because commercial producers had been using these methods with their grape juices all along.

Now we knew all we needed to make top-rate wines that cleared to brilliance of their own accord and which kept well. From this stage it has been only a story of progress. And it is ironical that after struggling for years in the dark, once we had brought daylight into our activities, the chief chemist of a famous British winery, who had known it all years before us, became interested and put a lot of useful information at our disposal. Helpful as he was, and grateful as we are to him, he understandably did not give nearly as much information as he might have done.

Learning as we did taught us more than any chemical encyclopaedia, talks or lectures could have done. After all, knowledge is useless without practical experience and learning the hard way is surely the most thorough training.

But our quest for perfection did not end here. In those changing times, tastes were also changing: most of us returning from the war had tasted some of the many foreign wines and I for one decided that it would be quite something if we could imitate them.

We had learned over our years of training that the grape was the only 'true' medium for making genuine wines. Any wine made from other materials was not wine in the strict meaning of the word, but was merely an imitation. The fact that it was excellent made no difference. This, in my view is bunkum – but there it is.

It is true that the grape is the best medium for fermentation. This is because it contains all the necessary elements of a thorough fermentation which wines of inferior quality lack; what is more, grapes usually contain these elements in the best proportions. Therefore, if we were to imitate commercially-produced wines we had, so far as we could, to introduce into our musts the chemical matter contained in grapes. Many English fruits do contain these elements in small quantities, so we had to make adjustments in some cases; where we used potatoes and other roots or grains such as wheat which contained none of the elements contained in grapes, we had to make wide and varied adjustments before we could hope to produce a must bearing any resemblance at all to one prepared from grapes.

Tannin, acids, sugar content, all had to be balanced and the recipe evolved after many trials. But we were still a long way from our goal. All kinds of fruit were tried and various methods, but always there was something lacking. For one thing we were not obtaining the fuller flavours, the bouquet we needed, nor the elusive vinous odour that makes for a quality wine. For it was real quality that we were seeking now, but we had only baker's yeast to work with.

Then came wine yeasts. By this time, there was actually a firm marketing them, unknown to us. These we tried at once with the Campden solution method already mentioned and the result was quality, quality all the way. But the story does not end there. Different yeasts gave different results with different fruit. So we had to find the yeast most suitable for the type of wine we wanted to make from the fruit we were using. More years of work were necessary before we were at last satisfied that we could set out to make a certain type of wine similar to a commercial product using English fruits in certain proportions and get the wine type we wanted. But when we could say before we began, 'This will be a good imitation of Beaujolais or Burgundy or Sauternes' or whatever, and then find it was as near to our goal as anyone is likely to get, we had, I thought, reached our zenith. But I was wrong. We are still learning about this subject, just as science is learning about space.

And so we have progressed from our primitive methods where failure was more likely than success to modern methods where success is certain. During all those years others were working on different lines from myself and my friends. Many people liked the flavours of wines made by the boiling method which produced those cloudy wines. Clarifying them was a problem they had to overcome, and they did this with the use of an enzyme which destroys the pectin in the fruit, thus preventing it holding minute solids in suspension to cloud the finished product. Starch-destroying enzymes are now also employed where starch-bearing ingredients such as roots and grains are used.

So now we use whichever method makes the kind of wine desired, without fuss or bother and with success assured.

1
WINE-MAKING:
BEFORE WE BEGIN

What a Recipe Amounts to

A recipe is basically a set of instructions to be followed under normal circumstances. There are good recipes and there are useless ones. But good or useless, a very great deal depends on the method used. A good recipe will make poor wine if it is used with an unsuitable method, while a poor recipe will make poor wine no matter what sort of method is used. Obviously, then, we want a good recipe with the most reliable and suitable method if we are to expect good results.

Wine-making, as I have said before, is rather like driving a car or, for that matter, doing anything that calls for a bit of commonsense. When learning to drive, you use someone else's recipe for driving. But when you have passed your test, you set about driving in your own way, bearing in mind what the instructor has instilled into you. If he was a good instructor, you will never forget the main essentials of driving because they will be instilled into you in the way that discipline is drilled into army recruits by a sergeant major.

And so it is with wine-making. You learn by the recipes of others and by your own mistakes. But what you learn on the way are the hard lessons that have to be learnt in anything that is worth doing well. And if there has ever been a subject worth learning it is wine-making, both for the results themselves and for the fascinating hobby that goes with them. If you learn about the technical background and understand the basic principles, you will be a far better wine- or beer-maker than if you follow recipes blindly without really understanding the whys and wherefores.

As you will see, a great deal goes on behind the scenes. There are a great many types and varieties of wines and beers, and it is for you to choose which one you want to make. The following recipes will take you near your goal. But when you have read and reread this book, you will have such a clear understanding of precisely what goes on behind the scenes that you will be able to look at wine- and beer-making in a different light. You will be able to vary recipes or dispense with them altogether and forge ahead confidently. Background knowledge of the subject will enable you to do this quite easily; without it, you would be completely stumped.

There is no need to alter or to try to balance any of the recipes in this book when using them for the first time, because they have been balanced already, so far as they can be. Also you do not have to use any equipment other than normal utensils for making wines or beers. My recipes make wines and beers as I like them and as a lot of other people like them. I am sure that you will like them too. But if you want a slight variation, wait until you have read and understood the technical details of this book and made wines or beers with the recipes, then you will know what to do.

A balanced recipe contains a list of all the ingredients necessary for a fully flavoured and, as far as is possible, a chemically balanced wine. It is imperative that the must we prepare contains all the essential elements for successful fermentation. In preparing a must we simulate, so far as we can, the chemical composition of grape juice. We do this because grape juice contains all the essential elements in the right proportions or near-right proportions for successful fermentation.

This is why we add acid and tannin to musts prepared from ingredients that do not contain them, such as roots, flowers and certain dried fruits. If we do not make up these deficiencies, fermentation would be unsatisfactory in many ways, and the wine would not be worth tasting, let alone drinking.

This is also why we use such small amounts of wild and garden fruits when we make wines with them. Usually they contain so much acid that, if we made wines with undiluted juice, we would not be able to drink them owing to the high acidity and in some cases astringency. So we take the simple way out by using what we consider to be the amount of fruit that will put into the must the amount of tannin and acid needed both for a good fermentation and a reasonably well-balanced wine.

The amount of fruit used is usually between 1.5 and 2.5kg (about 3-6 lb) depending on the type of wine – light, heavy, dry, sweet – required. But this is where a recipe can mislead.

During a normal to good season when fruits ripen well, the acidity is lessened and sugar content increased, and a good recipe will turn out good wines. But in a poor season when there has been a lot of rain and very little sunshine, the sugar content of the fruit will be very low and the acid content will be high. The wine produced will be totally different, apart from basic flavour, from the wine made in a good season, even though the same fruit and recipe are used. It is in such cases that background knowledge is so important for it enables you to make allowances for the differences in sugar and acid contents from season to season.

(12)

Other factors must also be taken into consideration, for example, soil conditions. Sand, clay and chalk all make a difference to the fruits in one way or another. Recipes cannot allow for this sort of thing. If you gather fruits from the same area every season there should be more consistency in their chemical balance than if they are gathered from widely differing places where each has been grown on different soils. There should be very little inconsistency in well-cultivated fruits from the same garden. But even here, you must allow for the unreliability of our climate. Anybody liking a particular type of wine made from wild or garden fruits would do well to cultivate these fruits in sufficient quantities for wine-making purposes.

You will now understand why you have been disappointed at odd times when using the same fruits with the same recipes.

Utensils and Apparatus

The choice of utensils is of far greater importance than is generally realized. Years ago, wine- and beer-makers were simply not catered for, so they had to use whatever they could lay their hands on. Very few of them realized that they were using utensils that caused spoilage in wines or that could turn out poisonous wines.

Today wine-makers have a wide choice of equipment. But that need not make it expensive; indeed, the initial outlay for making 5 or 10 l (1 or 2 gall) lots is quite small. Bear in mind that several 10 l (2 gall) batches a year add up to a nice amount of wine. If, like many, you drink your wines soon after they are made, then 25 l (5 gall) lots are more sensible. If you want to, you can make 50 or 100 l (10 or 20 gall) at a time. It is sound advice, however, to make 5 or 10 l (1 or 2 gall) batches to start with until you really get the feel of things. The initial outlay for the smaller batches is also more attractive.

Metals must, of course, be used when water, fruits or fruit juices are boiled. And they should be used for this purpose only. On no account should any metal be used for fermentation purposes. Also the fruits should be left in contact with metal for the shortest possible time. This is because fruit acids will attack any metal if they are in contact with it long enough. The result of this is discussed in Chapter 3 'Spoilage'.

The most suitable metals to use for boiling water and for fruits or juices are Monel metal, stainless steel, high-grade aluminium and, provided it is designed for cooking purposes, unchipped enamel. Enamel pails and similar utensils are not designed for cooking.

Fermentation should always be carried out in non-toxic polythene, glass or new stoneware. Barrels are suitable of course, provided that they are new or have been used for nothing except wine-making and that they are easily cleaned and sterilized. One of the greatest mistakes (and one I have myself been forced

(13)

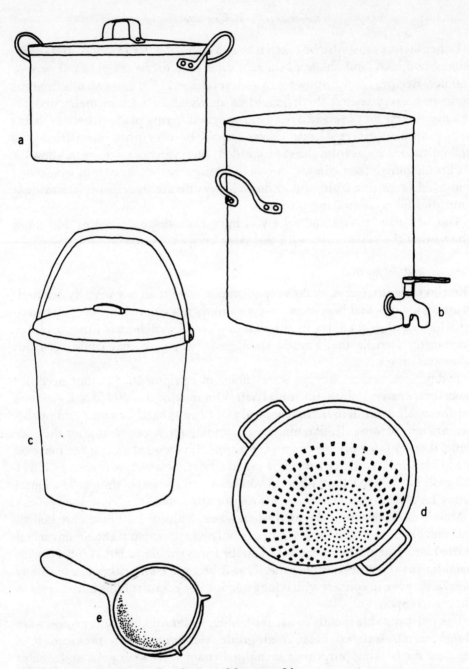

Utensils suitable for both wine- and beer-making
a Metal pan with lid and handles. For boiling worts in beer-making, or water and large amounts of fruits in wine-making.
b Metal pan with handles and tap. As above, but may also be used for sparging the grains in beer-making and running the sparge in to boiler or other container.
c Fermentation vessel   d Plastic colander   e Nylon and plastic sieve

to make owing to shortages years ago) is to use jars and barrels from other than a reliable dealer. How often has a wine-maker had an acquaintance tell him that if he likes to collect them there are half a dozen old stone jars 'up the end of the garden'. And how many unsuspecting wine-makers have gone after them like a shot.

Thank heaven we know better today. Even so, almost every week letters reach me from readers of my other books and of my magazine articles asking my opinion of the usefulness of certain vessels they have been given. Amongst these are old vinegar barrels, barrels that have contained vegetable oils or fruit juices and the like. Others write that they have acquired large plastic vessels of various shapes that have contained mild acids or other substances. Others confess that they have not the slightest idea what the vessels once contained.

In every case, for safety's sake I have advised throwing them away.

Containers that have held fruit juices, syrups or vegetable or cooking oils might be suitable if the nature of the plastic could be determined, and the containers cleaned so that they are safe. But as this is nigh on impossible, it is best not to use them. As for those that have contained acids of any sort, these should be destroyed. Many dangerous acids or deadly poisons are now available in plastic containers. Whether these could be safely cleaned and whether the plastic itself is suitable for our purposes is doubtful.

Glass containers that have contained fruit cordials or the larger vessels of distilled water are quite safe as these are easily sterilized. So if you know of a cheap source of supply of such vessels, take advantage of it.

Many hardware stores supply plastic vessels that might be considered suitable, but the assistant might not be able to tell you precisely the type of plastic used in its manufacture, and this is important. Alcohol produced during fermentation may attack the plasticizers used in plasticized PVC and similar vessels, so that the wine may become contaminated. Polythene, PVC (in which the plasticizer has not been used), terylene and nylon are quite suitable. But plastic vessels are not necessarily labelled as to what they are made of, and the assistant in the hardware store will often sell you anything without knowing what you want it for. In any case, he would not know whether it was suitable or not.

The straight-from-the-shoulder advice must therefore be, obtain your supplies from reliable firms dealing in your requirements. A list of these appears at the end of the book. Dealers in home wine-making and brewing ingredients and utensils hold large supplies of the utensils most suitable for our needs. Since they know precisely the type of vessel and the materials they should be made from, it goes without saying that these are the best people to go to. A wide range of sizes of all containers is available. All the wine-maker has to do is to decide in the light of the quantities he produces what size and type of vessel he needs.

A person setting out to make 5 l (1 gall) lots will need a 10 l (2 gall) polythene (or other suitable plastic) fermentation vessel, such as a pail, and a few one-gallon size glass jars for the secondary fermentation and for storage. Vessels for boiling the fruits or juices (where this is done) or for boiling the water will most likely already be in his kitchen. So he will need very little, apart from straining cloths, funnels of suitable plastic and fermentation locks (see p. 28). The more adventurous will need larger vessels of which there are plenty in the price lists of suppliers of home wine-making equipment.

There is no doubt that glass vessels are most popular for the secondary fermentation stage, and even for storage where red wines can be kept in the dark. Glass allows the operator to see what is going on.

For the home brewer, there are polythene dustbins for mashing and fermenting purposes. Being lightweight and unbreakable, they are very popular. (Those making draught beers will have to use stone tap-hole jars for storage. They are rather expensive but need only be bought once. And you will need only two or three because they are emptied a week or two after being filled.)

Although in my view it is an insult to wines to put them into vessels shaped like a jerry-can, there is no doubt that this type of plastic vessel is becoming increasingly popular for the secondary fermentation stage and for storage purposes. They are unbreakable, light, and easy to carry about.

So, before you buy new utensils or replace old ones, have a good look through several price lists, or better still visit your nearest supplier to see just what is available; you will be surprised, I am sure.

Measures

While on the subject of utensils, a word about measuring is timely. It is well worthwhile making sure that jugs or other vessels are graduated in litres or pints, up to near the rim. Small liquid measures are usually marked for teaspoons and tablespoons. And bear in mind that these are recognized measures. So do not use a teaspoon or tablespoon from the cutlery drawer because they are likely to be wide of the true measure. How often one reads in recipes of the need for a level teaspoonful or tablespoonful of such and such. Yet there are a dozen different sizes of teaspoons and tablespoons.

Therefore use a proper measure and work more safely – especially when you are measuring acid or some constituent that will have a very marked effect upon the flavour of the wine.

A word about metrication It will be seen that in all the recipes our popular pounds and ounces measures are given together with the metric equivalents. The latter, however, have of necessity been rounded up where this was found to be inevitable. The figures quoted bear with the Government's recommended table – a copy of which appears on this page.

Most of you will use the pound and ounces figures as you have always done. Those using the metric equivalents, as the younger readers will, will find that all utensils for wine- and beer-making today are marked in the various measures tables.

Smaller vessels are marked in fluid ounce-tablespoons and cubic centimetres, so that they may be used for whichever measures scale you prefer. So do bear in mind that a tablespoon is an accurate measure (but use the proper tablespoon-fluid ounce measuring vessel and *not* a tablespoon from the cutlery drawer). I make this point because there are several different sized tablespoons in that cutlery drawer. In the chapter on flower wines it was decided to leave the pint and quart measures to stand, simply because these measures have been used for centuries and nobody to date has ever bothered to weigh a quart of dandelion heads or whatever it is. But jugs with quarts measures together with the metric equivalents will be available for years to come – so that nobody should experience any difficulty.

Metric Conversion Table

1 gall	5 l	1 lb	450 g
1 pt	6 dl	½ lb	225 g
½ pt	3 dl	¼ lb	100 g
¼ pt	1.5 dl	2 oz	50 g
6 tbs	1 dl	1 oz	25 g
		½ oz	15 g

Corking

Just let me say that I have never yet found the need to use a corking machine. This is because I always used the flanged (flat-topped, mushroom-shaped) corks with a plastic seal. They are quite cheap and are best bought by the gross. The seals are slipped over the top of the cork at bottling time, pressed down all round and allowed to dry out. As they do so in an hour or so, they shrink to form an airtight seal and become very, very tight after a while. They are easily removed when the wine is required.

A word about storing these seals. They come in airtight cans filled with fluid. Once the can has been opened, I like to turn the lot into a small Kilner jar or other screwtop jar of about 450 g (1 lb) size. Some instant coffee jars are ideal, but bear in mind that the jar must be kept airtight, otherwise the fluid that keeps the seals expanded will evaporate, and the seals shrink and become useless.

I have covered all the essential equipment in this section. If you are pressed into buying non-essentials, your wine- and beer-making will become expensive. So get the bare essentials to start with, and you will see then that you have everything you need.

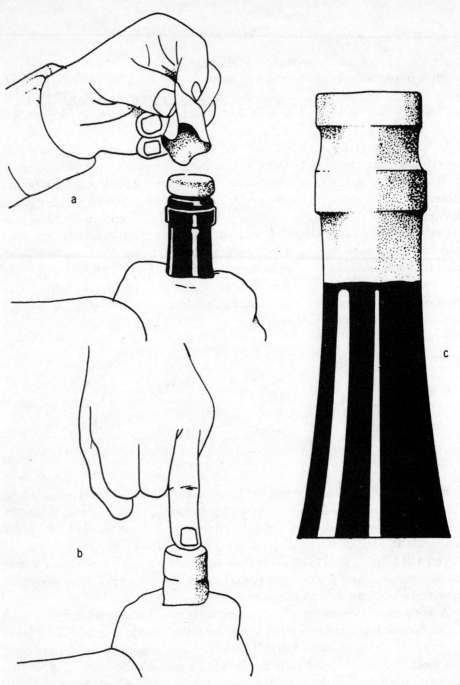

Corking and fitting plastic seals

a Slip the plastic seal over the cork.

b Press the seal very firmly all round. It will be oversize for a while, but soon shrinks to fit.

c The shrunken seal forming an airtight fit.

2
FERMENTATION

This is the process which turns our musts (prepared mixtures) into wine. Without fermentation, they would remain more or less as we prepared them, for a short time at least. If we did not add suitable yeast, but merely left the prepared mixture to itself, fermentation of sorts would commence. And undoubtedly this would be caused by a mixture of undesirable yeasts and bacteria which were on the fruits when we prepared the must or which came into contact with it later. This aspect is covered more fully in Chapter 3 'Spoilage'.

An enormous amount of study and research has been and still is being done on the process of fermentation. A century ago it was barely understood; indeed, yeast was not generally accepted as the medium which brought about fermentation. Today we could not hope to make wines without special yeast. By this I do not mean expensive yeast but selected yeast. There are countless varieties of yeast as we see under 'Spoilage', but the yeasts we use to make wines must be pure. They must not be contaminated with wild, or undesirable yeast. Every possible care is taken to ensure that the yeasts we buy are suitable for our purpose and as pure as modern processes will allow.

Yeast, it may surprise many, is a living organism. When obtained it is inactive, or dormant.

To produce wines from the musts we prepare we add yeast of a special type and give it the means not only to become active, but also to live and reproduce itself. In return, it produces a number of by-products, the main one being alcohol. In addition, glycerine, acetaldehyde and other substances are produced in quite minute quantities. Yet these are important to the fullness or completeness of fermentation.

It has been found that enzymes (see p. 21) secreted by the yeast cells bring about the all-important changes necessary for full and complete fermentation. It seems that yeast, given suitable conditions, will produce the enzymes that it

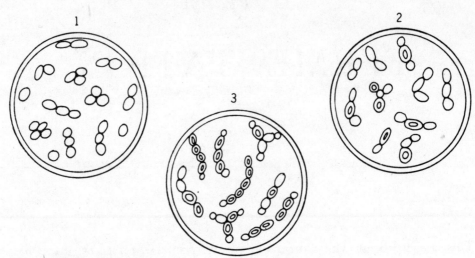

Yeast under microscope
The illustration shows how the yeast cells multiply.

needs to take itself through all the necessary stages of fermentation. As one enzyme completes its work, it stops (becomes inactive) to allow another to take over. If this were not the case, too much of certain substances, and not enough of others, would be produced. But this does not happen.

All in all, yeast and the enzymes it produces form a complex system complete in itself, relying only on the means of sustaining itself. And this it does on the sugar we put into the must. But if we give it too much sugar to begin with its reaction is slow and erratic, or perhaps it will not react at all. Hence the general desirability of starting our ferments at a specific gravity of not more than 1.110 (for more about this see Chapter 5 'The Hydrometer'). Hence also the need to produce in the must a certain amount of acid, tannin and other desirable matter.

As already mentioned, yeast is dormant when purchased. If we add it to the must in this state, we may have to wait several days for it to become active. So we make what we call a nucleus ferment. In doing this we produce a colony of active yeasts which, when put into a prepared must, will start the must into active fermentation almost immediately. The overriding importance of this is that the prepared must is not left open for a day or so to attacks by wild yeasts and bacteria. Even when covered as directed in the methods, a must where there is no fermentation going on is open to attack because there is not a constant stream of carbon dioxide gas (CO_2) escaping through the puckers of the tied-down covering to keep out the air.

This brings me to the importance of what we call fermenting under anaerobic conditions – fermenting in the absence of atmospheric oxygen. Years ago, at the age of five, I was introduced to home-made wines by falling head first into a tub of fermenting dandelions in my grandfather's outhouse. And, alas, until recently open fermentation was still practised. Yeast creates anaerobic conditions for itself to a certain degree, but it cannot prevent the escape of the gas it produces. By covering fermenting wines with tied-down sheet polythene, we can control the release of the gas and leave the wine fermenting with a protective cloud of carbon dioxide gas above it.

Later we put the fermenting wines under fermentation locks (see p. 28), usually at the stage where the fermentation has slowed down and where the gas being produced would no longer be sufficient to form a protective cloud.

From all this it will be seen at once that yeast produces not only all the essentials for a full and complete fermentation, but also its own protection from wild yeasts and bacteria so far as it can. When the yeast leaves off, we take over in order to safeguard it and the wine we are preparing.

But whatever happens during fermentation, most amateurs are concerned mainly with the production of alcohol, flavour and bouquet.

When using English wild and garden fruits we cannot use enough to produce in a must the amount of sugar needed to make the amount of alcohol we want, simply because these fruits contain so little sugar and so much acid and tannin that the wines would be undrinkable owing to the high acidity and astringency. For example, to put into a must enough natural fruit sugar we might need as much as 35 kg (80 lb) of blackberries, plums or whatever we might be using – and nobody would be able to drink it if that amount of fruit were used to make 5 l (1 gall) of wine.

So when we use, say, 1.5-2.5 kg of fruit to 5 l (about 4-6 lb per gall) in order to obtain as near as possible the strength of flavour we need (not forgetting roughly the amount of acid and tannin we need as well), there is a grave shortage of sugar. Obviously, with so little fruit being used, the amount of fruit sugar in a must will be very small, enough perhaps to make about 1 or 2% of alcohol. And since good wines require alcohol in the region of 15% by volume, we must obviously add sugar to produce the type of wine we want and the amount of alcohol we want it to contain.

Here it is important to understand the meaning of alcohol tolerance of yeasts. In general, we use the word 'tolerate' to mean the limit of our endurance or 'the amount we can put up with'. So we can call the maximum tolerance of yeast 'the amount of alcohol it can put up with'. And this is in the region of 15% by volume. When this level is reached the yeast is destroyed by the alcohol, no more fermentation takes place and no more alcohol is made.

When yeast is added to a must, its first action is to convert the household sugar we add to 'invert sugar'. This is brought about by an enzyme in the yeast known as invertase. This change is necessary because yeast cannot ferment cane sugar in the form in which it is usually added. Having done this, the yeast almost at once begins to reproduce itself. Each yeast cell – so tiny that something like one thousand of them could queue across a penny – sends out a bud which in turn sends out another bud, and so on. At certain stages the cell looks something like a deformed potato.

During this reproduction process the yeast feeds upon the sugar, turning approximately half into alcohol and half into carbon dioxide gas. It is in the early stages of yeast reproduction that fermentation is very vigorous and the production of alcohol is quite high. The colony of yeast continues to reproduce millions of new cells as others die. Initially the production of new yeasts exceeds the death of others, so that we have an increasing number of yeast cells hour by hour.

After a while the rate slows down, and it is at this stage that those who evolve methods and recipes, as I do myself, recommend putting the wine under fermentation locks (see p. 28). We judge as nearly as possible when this is likely to be necessary and include the instruction in the method in the hope that the individual operator's must will react as we expect it to. Sometimes it does not, and we receive indignant letters from readers whose wines are climbing out of the jars through the fermentation lock. Fortunately these happenings are rare. The slowing-down of fermentation is increased by using a fermentation lock because we cut off the oxygen supply. This causes the yeast to turn to the sugar for its oxygen, thus using up more sugar and producing a little more alcohol than if it obtained its oxygen from outside.

After a fermentation lock has been fitted, we usually regard the wine as having stepped into the secondary fermentation stage, although there is no clear distinction between the primary and secondary stages, because the two overlap. By secondary, we mean, in general, the less vigorous fermentation that goes on for several weeks, according to the composition of the must, temperature and other factors which have bearing on the length of fermentation.

Composition of the Must

A reasonably well-balanced must made up from a good recipe will contain all the essentials for full and complete fermentation. Until a few years ago, hardly any amateur had heard of yeast nutrients which we now add in order to help the yeast to make the maximum alcohol.

I have said that yeast and the enzymes it produces form a complex system capable of producing its own needs to take it through fermentation. This is true as regards the enzymes needed for this purpose. But yeast needs more than that to give it the basis from which to work. The yeast can reproduce itself on sugar alone, but if it is to continue to do this and survive the strength of alcohol it produces it must have other things as well. If it does not get them, fermentation is likely to stop early on so that perhaps only 8% or 9% of alcohol by volume or less is made. (See 'Sticking Ferments', p. 31.)

English wild and garden fruits undoubtedly contain most of the essential needs of the yeast. But bear in mind that we dilute these juices to such an extent that these essentials are reduced practically to insignificance, in the same way as the sugar they contain. To make up for this dilution we add the essential substances in the form of chemical nutrients, just as we add sugar.

A good nutrient will contain a balanced consortium of all the chemicals the yeast is likely to need and certainly those in which our greatly diluted musts are deficient. Several important chemicals will be found in sufficient quantity even in greatly diluted musts. But generally we must add ammonium sulphate, magnesium sulphate (Epsom salts) and pottassium phosphate. All of these, with certain additives, are contained in a good nutrient.

Temperature

This is another important factor affecting fermentation. And although some writers on the subject recommend a figure as high as 26°C (80°F), I have found that a reasonably constant temperature in the region of 18° to 21°C (65° to 70° F) is perfectly satisfactory.

Making wines all the year round is quite simple these days. But it used to be almost impossible in the old days. Wines made in late summer or early autumn almost always stopped fermenting on the first cold night of late autumn or early winter. This resulted in the wine-maker thinking that his wine had ceased altogether. And so he bunged it down to clear and, when ready, bottled it as a finished product. When a warm spell, in February or perhaps a bit later, penetrated to the yeast, it became active again and began to make the amount of alcohol it would have made if the cold had not prevented it.

This meant that corks or bungs flew out, and the wine clouded as yeast was brought into suspension by the agitation of renewed fermentation. Many wine-makers thought their wines had gone wrong and threw them away. Others did go wrong because the blown bungs were not noticed and the wines were left uncovered and therefore open to attack by wild yeasts and bacteria. This is covered more fully in Chapter 3 'Spoilage'.

Today all these troubles are a thing of the past because we can use thermostatically controlled heaters to keep our wines at the correct temperature. They can be installed quite cheaply and are inexpensive to run. (See the section on the fermentation cupboard, p. 33.) This enables fermentation to go on unhindered throughout the coldest weather and ensures trouble-free wine-making with the maximum alcohol being made without undue problems. Trouble-free continuous fermentation is of the utmost importance for top-quality results; flavour, bouquet and all-round quality depends on this.

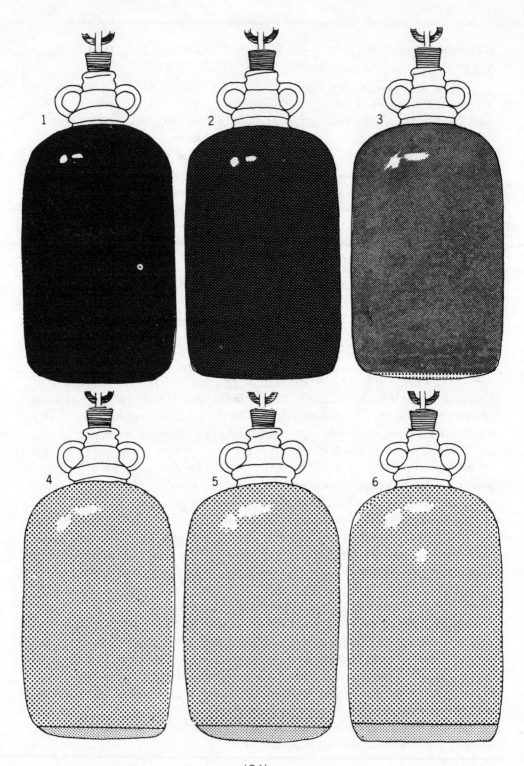

Fermentation

How wines become clear

1 When wine is first put into a jar it is so cloudy that it is impossible to see through it.
2 As the yeast and other solids begin to settle out the wine appears far less muddy.
3 You should just be able to see through the wine at this stage.
4 Now much clearer.
5 There should only be hazes to settle out now.
6 The brilliant wine ready for siphoning off the yeast deposit.

It is important to understand that wines do not normally become brilliantly clear until fermentation has ceased. If they do, then your luck is in. But on the whole it is wise never to expect wines to become brilliant until a few weeks after fermentation has ceased, as while fermentation is going on, the upsurge of gas keeps minute particles of fruit and the yeast in suspension, distributed throughout the wine.

As fermentation slows down, there is less gas rising, so the heavier particles settle to the bottom of the jar while the almost weightless solids are kept in suspension. Slowly, very slowly, fermentation loses its vigour, and slowly the almost weightless solids begin to settle too. But the wine will still remain hazy for quite some time. If a good yeast and a method is used that does not allow for pectin or starch to hold solids in suspension, the wine should become brilliant a couple of weeks after fermentation stops.

What to expect when making red wines. When the still fermenting wine is put into a jar and the fermentation lock fitted the wine will be very cloudy, and at this stage it will be impossible to see through the jar even if held to bright light. This will last until fermentation begins to slow, although you will notice a slight deposit forming in the jar. Wines that will be dark red when clear – elderberry, blackberry, black plum, whortleberry, and a few others such as those made with Burgundy concentrate – will begin to lose their pink hue and take on a darker colour. The deposit in the jar will gradually become thicker, perhaps a quarter of an inch thick. This process will continue until about half-way through fermentation when it will be possible to see through the jar when held to light. And from then on the darkening of the wine will continue as the wines become clearer. The darkening takes place because the particles causing the pinkness are settling out. When all particles have settled the wine is its normal colour and brilliantly clear.

Wines that will be a whisky colour when clear – made from oranges, certain concentrated grape juices, and roots or dried fruit – are often a sandy brown and look quite dirty when first put into a jar and one doubts whether this filthy-looking stuff will ever clear. But they react in the same way as the red. As the particles settle out the wine slowly takes on the colour of whisky – but not until all fermentation has ceased, or perhaps a week or two later.

Wines that will be pale gold to pink will often look pathetically anaemic, but this is quite natural. As fermentation slows the wine's true colour begins to show, and when fermentation has ceased and the last of the solids are firmly on the bottom of the jar the wine above is such a delicious looking pale gold or pink that you will want to drink it straightaway.

Wines that will be only slightly coloured – most root and flower wines – often look like off-white milk when first put into a jar. The milkiness is caused by the paleness of the wine and the pale-coloured yeast held in suspension by the upsurge of gas. As fermentation nears completion, the palest of gold, the pastel pink or the pure white of the wine will appear, and in a few weeks you will have a brilliantly clear wine.

So don't worry about those murky wines. Be patient and all will be well.

(25)

As mentioned, we rarely add yeast in its dormant state because of the delay before it becomes active. In preparing a nucleus in the following manner, we are able to have a small batch of yeast already fermenting to add to a prepared must. I am aware, of course, that a great many people use yeast successfully without preparing a nucleus, but there will always be those who confound the critics.

Making a Nucleus

Many proprietory yeasts are supplied with directions for making a nucleus, but there are no hard and fast rules except that it should be reasonably balanced. By this, I do not mean that each little part of it must be measured. What I mean is that we should use a fruit juice, which, for all intents and purposes, may be regarded as balanced when diluted with a little water and sugar. Lemon, orange or any other fruit juice, or diluted fruit syrups such as Ribena are all perfectly satisfactory. Even diluted malt extract is suitable. But if we use this, we must add a little acid and tannin as well.

You can make a good nucleus with .3 dl (1 fl oz) of any fruit juice and 1.5 dl (5 fl oz) of water in which 50 g (2 oz) of sugar have been boiled. If the juice is lemon or orange, add a tablespoon of strong tea as well to make up the deficiency of tannin in the citrus fruits. Add the yeast to the liquid and pour it into a small narrow-necked bottle. Plug the neck with a firm knob of cotton wool to protect it against the ingress of wild yeast and bacteria.

The ideal type of bottle to use for your nucleus is the sort of baby-feed bottle that can be boiled. Having watched my grandchildren being fed, I decided that if the hole in the teat were made from inside with a needle, the teat itself filled with cotton wool and then fitted to the bottle with its screw cap, the nucleus would be adequately protected; the gas can escape through that tiny hole and the cotton wool plug will prevent the ingress of spoilage organisms until the yeast begins to ferment and so form its own protective barrier of carbon dioxide gas.

If you do not want to use this sort of bottle some other sort will do, but the neck must be closed with a knob of cotton wool. In this case you should run a lighted match round the cotton wool before removing it to destroy any wild yeast or bacteria that might be trapped in it. Shake the bottle before adding the nucleus to the must.

Adding a colony of active yeast is a great benefit. It means that the prepared must is in active fermentation in a matter of hours, whereas in many cases, depending on the type of yeast used, it may be three or four days before fermentation gets under way, thus leaving the must exposed, even though it may be covered, to attacks by wild yeasts and bacteria. Not all yeasts require to be made into a nucleus. Many added in their dry state will have the must in active fermentation in an hour or so. It is all a matter of choosing the best yeast for your purpose, although I have found that those requiring to be made into a nucleus usually produce the better-quality wines.

Stages of Fermentation

Fermentation is seen as a frothing on the surface of the must, accompanied by a gentle hissing or fizzing which is quite audible. There is also a pleasant smell which is often quite different from the smell one would expect the fruits being fermented to give off.

During the first few days, fermentation is usually very vigorous, the wine becoming warmed by energy produced by the yeast. Furthermore, where fruits are being fermented, the pips and skins rise to form a cake upon the surface. For this reason it is wise to allow several inches of headroom in the fermenting vessel. When juices only are fermented, a heavy frothing will appear.

The secondary fermentation stage is often regarded as imminent when the cake of skins levels off to flatness and when the froth of a juice ferment peters out, leaving the surface reasonably free from froth. When the heavier part of the cake of skins has sunk and the frothing of a juice ferment has completely stopped, it is reasonable to assume that the secondary fermentation has begun.

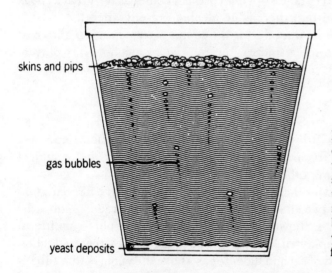

skins and pips

gas bubbles

yeast deposits

Pips and skins form a cake on the surface during the vigorous fermentation stage. They are brought up by the upsurge of millions of tiny gas bubbles produced by the yeast during fermentation.

It is at this stage, regardless of directions to the contrary in methods, that the fruits should be pressed free of juice and the wine strained into a jar to be put under a fermentation lock. Juice ferments are treated similarly but need no straining. During the stage under fermentation locks fermentation continues slowly but surely and the amount of alcohol increases accordingly.

(27)

Do not be worried by prolonged fermentation. Indeed a long, steady fermentation is of great importance in producing good-quality wines.

It is safe to say that all the time the solution on the lock is pushed up to the out-going side, a little fermentation is still going on, regardless of whether bubbles are passing through or not. It must be borne in mind that the longer fermentation continues, the more alcohol is produced and this alcohol has a weakening effect upon the yeast. This effect continues until the maximum amount of alcohol the yeast can tolerate is finally reached. At this stage the whole complex yeast system is destroyed, and, as we have seen, fermentation ceases. The last of the minute solids forming slight hazes settle out now that there is no longer any disturbance caused by yeast action to keep them in suspension.

Many people tend to become worried by a slow fermentation and either increase the temperature or lower it in the hope of creating more favourable conditions of the yeast. Both these courses are unwise. First, overheating can destroy the yeast and harm the must. Secondly, lowering the temperature to any great extent can cause the yeast to go dormant.

In both cases, restarting the yeast may be very difficult and attempts are often quite futile. Even adding new yeast or some of the original nucleus may fail simply because the percentage of alcohol present comes as too great a shock to the yeast. Bear in mind that there is no alcohol present when the yeast is normally added to a must and that, during the course of fermentation, the yeast becomes accustomed to an ever-increasing amount of alcohol. But putting yeast into a must already containing say, 10% to 11% of alcohol, is a very different matter.

The Fermentation Lock

There is no doubt that this little piece of equipment is one of the most important in the wine-maker's armoury, and it is a pity that certain writers on this subject tend to lead people to think otherwise.

When the wine is racked for the first time and then put into jars, fermentation locks are fitted as a matter of course. Sterilizing solution is poured in to the level shown and fermentation is allowed to proceed under anaerobic conditions. This state is, as already explained, created by the yeast itself by the production of a heavier-than-air cloud of carbon dioxide gas above the wine. A thin tube of glass stuffed with cotton wool would allow the excess gas to escape and would prevent the ingress of bacteria, insects and moulds which cause the wines to spoil.

If this were all that is needed, then fermentation locks could be dispensed with. But this is not so. Bear in mind that fermentation locks are used during what we call the secondary fermentation stage and, as we have seen, this is the

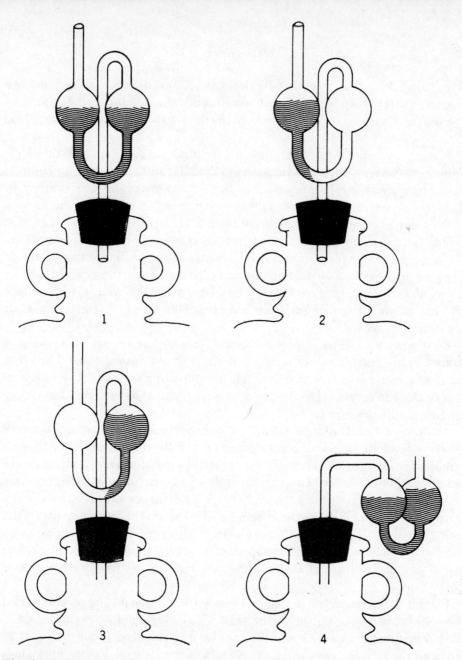

The fermentation lock

Fig. 1 shows a fermentation lock fitted to a jar and filled with sterilising solution to the usual level.

Fig. 2 shows the position of the solution as a bubble of gas is about to pass through it.

Fig. 3 shows how a fermentation lock sometimes works in reverse.

Fig. 4. This type of lock is very useful where little headroom is available, such as in a small fermentation cupboard. The one drawback of this type is that, because little sterilising solution can be put in, frequent topping-up is necessary to prevent the lock drying out.

stage where fermentation gradually slows down. It is during the slowing down that some sort of trap is necessary to retain sufficient gas and at the same time release the excess. This function is performed admirably by the sterilizing solution in the fermentation lock.

Water would suffice for this purpose were it not for some special considerations. First, water cannot remain pure indefinitely, and any moulds or bacteria that might come into contact with it would automatically contaminate it. Indeed, I have seen wine flies actually drown themselves in the water in the lock in their desperate efforts to reach the wine under its protection.

During the quite vigorous ferment that usually goes on for a few days after the lock is fitted, the see-saw action of the water could mean that a tiny amount might be thrown far back and find its way down the stem of the lock and into the jar. And if this water were already contaminated, the wine might well be affected. So using sterilizing solution is the best plan, for any bacteria or moulds are destroyed by it.

Further, it sometimes happens that the pressure in the jar falls owing to sudden cold contracting the wine, and air is drawn into the jar. The air is purified because it has to pass through the sterilizing solution. The lock is in fact working in reverse. This occurrence is nothing to worry about, but it does tend to puzzle newcomers.

Apart from the advantages already described, the fermentation lock is a very good guide to the rate of fermentation. This is indicated by the rate at which bubbles are seen passing through. Early on, they may form an almost continuous stream, but later fermentation slows down and bubbles are observed only at long intervals. Later still, there may be no evidence that fermentation is continuing except for the solution being pushed up on the out-going side of the lock. A gas bubble might pass through every one or two hours, but because no one can watch it for this long there appears to be no activity at all. It is therefore sound practice to leave the wine under the lock all the time the solution is pushed up.

Later it will be observed that after a slow fermentation lasting several weeks, the solution is drawn up the wrong side. The lock should be examined daily after this in order to note when the solution has returned to normal, that is, when all the solution remains at the bottom of the U-bend. When this state is observed, it is safe to say that fermentation has ceased.

Users of the hydrometer (see Chapter 5) will know for sure by taking the reading to ascertain whether or not the maximum alcohol for the type of wine being made has been reached. Those not using the hydrometer are advised to leave the wine under locks and in a warm place for three or four weeks before regarding it safe to rack and set aside for storing. This is advised for the very simple reason that, although the lock indicates that fermentation has ceased, there can still be a few yeast spores not yet killed that can carry on the fermentation for a few days longer.

When using the type of fermentation lock illustrated it is advisable to insert a small plug of cotton wool in the open end in order to give double protection to the wine. The solution, which will slowly lose its strength, should be replenished from time to time. There is no need to remove the lock for this, merely add a few drops with an eye dropper or pipette.

Glass locks are often difficult to insert and remove from bungs. To ease this situation, merely moisten the stem with water or sterilizing solution. Rubber bungs take a mighty grip on the stem of locks that have been in jars for months on end. Twisting to remove the locks will break the fragile glass. To break the grip, immerse lock and bung in water for a few minutes. The bung will then slide off easily.

Sticking Ferments

When we say that fermentation has stuck we mean that it has stopped prematurely. In other words, it has stopped before the yeast has made all the alcohol that it can. There are a number of reasons for this.

But first, do not pay too much attention to the fact that fermentation ceases or appears to have ceased just after the fermenting wine is put into a fresh container – for example, when it is poured from the fermentation pail into the jar to be put under a fermentation lock. I say this because there is quite often a break in fermentation at this stage, though I will admit that there should not be. Either way, if this happens it will be found that fermentation is on the go again within a few hours as a rule.

Our main concern must be with ferments when they stop without apparent cause, resulting in a sweet wine where a dry was required or an over-sweet wine when a normally sweet wine was the aim.

Now let me say that once fermentation has begun it should continue unhindered until the maximum alcohol the yeast can make is actually made. So if it stops we must try to find the cause.

Years ago the main cause was the first cold night of autumn. Wines made during late summer and early autumn would ferment vigorously enough until that first cold night when it stopped. The inexperienced hobbyist, noting that the wine had finished, bunged it down and put it away as a finished product, doubtless looking forward to the time when he could proudly bottle it and offer it to friends. But when a mild spell during winter or the first real warm days of spring turned up the yeast, stirred by the warmth, recommenced fermenting where it left off. I often wonder how many thousands of gallons of good wines were poured down the sink through this, for the same inexperienced hobbyist, seeing his once clear wine heavily clouded and not tasting very nice, thought that calamity had struck. All that in fact needs to be done if this happens is to bring the wine into the warm, fit a fermentation lock and leave it until all fermentation has ceased again. Actually, although this sort of thing can be a confounded nuisance, it is a blessing in disguise for the simple reason that a far better wine is the outcome. The simplest means of preventing cold stopping fermentation is to make a fermentation cupboard as described on p. 33.

Now, a well-balanced must – that is, one containing all the essentials for a full and complete fermentation – will not stop fermenting prematurely unless interfered with unduly. So many people rack (transfer their wines from one container to another) every couple of weeks or so, when the rule should be to leave it alone. In my methods the first stage of fermentation is carried on in the fermenting pail where many of the fruit or vegetable particles are strained out after a short time. The second short period in the pail is to allow the lighter solids and much of the yeast to settle during a somewhat slower ferment. When the wine is put into a jar with the instruction in the method to leave as much of the muddy deposit in the pail as you can, you leave behind what would normally build up as sediment in the jar, so there is no need for further racking until fermentation has ceased. In this way we avoid undue disturbance and the risk of stopping fermentation too soon. It is a fact that if fermentation stops at around 12% of alcohol you are not likely to get it going again. New yeast is likely to be killed by the amount of alcohol already present so there is no point in adding any. The result is that what should have been a dry wine is sweet and what should have been a nicely sweet wine is quite syrupy. And you will have to put up with it or blend it as described on p.52. One means of avoiding trouble of this sort is to make sure you obtain a good yeast, and your local wine supply shop will tell you which is the most popular.

Setting the wine near a boiler where the temperature fluctuates from day to day, or in the airing cupboard, is asking for trouble because there can be no control of temperature. Overheating is just as troublesome as a cold night. Where central heating is installed there is no problem and the spare bedroom is often pressed into use for fermentation purposes. The fact is that a constant temperature of around 18°C (65°F) is ideal. So it all boils down to using a reliable recipe that puts into the must all the essentials of a full and complete fermentation with a reliable method, a good yeast and nutrient, keeping the wine warm and leaving it undisturbed until the maximum alcohol is reached.

Many hobbyists use the airing cupboard to keep their fermenting wines warm and provided it does not become overheated, as it very easily can, it often proves satisfactory up to a point. But there are bound to be variations of temperature and at odd times when the fire dies down or goes out, or the electricity supply is switched off, the temperature will fall quite rapidly. This can only result in an erratic fermentation, rapid one day, slow the next; anyone looking at the fermentation lock daily to see how fermentation is progressing might well be puzzled because bubbles will be few one day and many the next and so on. So the airing cupboard is not the best place after all. Overheating will stop fermentation just as surely as a sudden drop in temperature.

Many people use special fermentation pails fitted with a lid containing two holes, one for the wire of an immersion heater of the sort used in tropical fish tanks and another for a fermentation lock. These may well work admirably for some people, but the experience I have had with them was not encouraging. Special trays with an electric element completely encased within it can prove useful. The pail or the jars of wine may be stood in this and the warmth from the tray warms the wine from the base upwards.

Fermentation is often stopped during cool to cold weather if the wine is poured from the fermenting pail (as in the methods) when the jar is cold. This can chill the wine and therefore the yeast. To prevent this during cold weather, fill the jar with hot water – but not hot enough to crack the jar – and let it stand for a few minutes so that the glass absorbs the heat. Then empty and sterilize quickly before filling with wine.

We use nutrients which are included in the recipes and methods and these do assist fermentation, but no more should be added if fermentation sticks. However the addition of a vitamin B tablet will often assist in getting fermentation on the go again. One thing I have not mentioned that will stop fermentation is unnecessary racking – transferring wine to another vessel without good reason. Many people do this each month. I never rack more than once and that is when the wine is put into the jar and the deposit is left in the pail. From then on, the wine is left to finish fermenting *undisturbed*. If there is a thick deposit of about 10 mm (⅜ in), I rack into another jar before storing. But there should not be more than 3-6 mm (⅛-¼ in) of deposit in the jar when fermentation ceases and this can be left until the wine is brilliantly clear which in the normal way is only a week or two.

The Fermentation Cupboard

In my many other books on this subject I recommend using a fermentation cupboard and even in these days of rocketing fuel costs it is still worthwhile because consumption of fuel is negligible.

So many people have written to me from time to time asking for some idea of what a fermentation cupboard really amounts to that I am giving a few details here. Almost any cupboard can be converted into a fermentation cupboard. The 'handy-carpenter-sort-of-bloke' would have no trouble in making one to fit into a given space. About the only really important point is the shelving which should be similar to that used in airing cupboards and set in a similar fashion to allow for free movement of warmth. Bear in mind that a 5l (1 gall)

(33)

jar of wine weighs about 6 kg (14 lb), so the timber will have to be strong. Another important point is that the distance between the shelving should be ample to allow for a jar of wine plus the lock to be moved in and out without knocking the lock to smithereens on the shelf above. Old kitchen cabinets, wardrobes and such like can easily be converted to a fermentation cupboard.

One point I think I should mention here is that you should make the cupboard bigger than you will need to start with because as you really get under way you will need quite a bit of space.

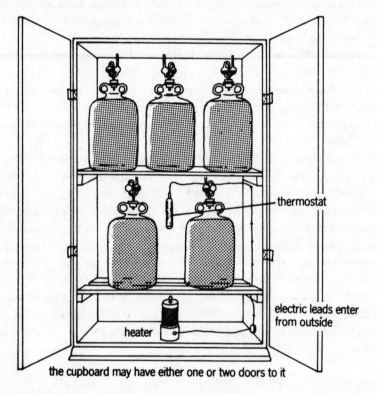

the cupboard may have either one or two doors to it

The fermentation cupboard
This is rather small but it does illustrate what is required.

The illustration shows only five jars, but it will give you a rough idea of how to go about making something bigger. The heater illustrated is known as a 100w black heater (it does not become red like an electric fire) and is supplied complete with a thermostat set at 21°C (70°F) which is quite satisfactory. There are larger sorts and other fittings. I think Loftus, whose address appears at the end of the book, is the only firm supplying these. If you have made wines previously and had sticking ferments you will know what a blessing a fermentation cupboard will be. But while on this subject, I think it wise and only right to bring to your notice the fact that certain yeasts will ferment perfectly satisfactorily and quite quickly, I am assured, even in fairly cold conditions. Unfortunately at the time of writing, I have not had time to carry out trials with these yeasts, but I understand that they come from the Vierka range marketed mainly by Semplex whose address appears at the end of this book.

Having made wines for over thirty-five years and watched the growth of practically every aspect of the hobby and some of the wild claims made for various ingredients and 'items' (I apologize for being vague but I cannot be otherwise here) I have become sceptical. Anyway, on a recent visit to a wine-making circle I engineered a situation where I might have first-hand recommendation for these yeasts which, I must admit, quite a number of people have been using with great success. One fellow was so enthusiastic about these yeasts that he offered me wines made with them and went on to explain that the three I tried had been fermented to dryness in under one month. A sweet wine would, of course, need a week or two longer. The wines were excellent and one in particular had fermented right out in just under three weeks. He still uses the fermentation cupboard he made years ago, but without any heat now.

All this is most remarkable, and because two other members of that same circle confirmed that the fellow was being perfectly honest I had no alternative but to accept what he told me. And I must admit that I, who must keep one stride ahead in this business if I possibly can, had fallen many paces behind. So I do urge you to try these cold fermenting yeasts for yourself and if you do not happen to be as successful as my informant you can always fall back on a fermentation cupboard. These yeasts do, incidentally, ferment well in a temperature of 5-10°C (40-50°F) which is, I should imagine, the normal temperature of an unheated room except in the coldest part of the winter.

3
SPOILAGE:
PREVENTION AND
CURE

Spoilage

When you realize the number of troubles that can beset the wine-maker, you might well ask how on earth he ever manages to make good wines. The simple answer is that he has come to realize that prevention of troubles is better than attempts to cure the result, and he works accordingly. Therefore he has no trouble.

But there are people making wines who often have them turn to vinegar; go insipid and flat; take on odours that have nothing to do with the decomposition of vegetable matter and dead yeast cells; become sharp or apparently over-acid on storage; have medicinal flavours; become thick and oily; become harsh of flavour and assume an overpowering or sickly bouquet; or become sickly sweet to the palate. All these troubles, besides a few that are peculiar to individual wine-makers, are quite easily avoided. But without understanding the causes, no one would know the preventive measures that are necessary.

Most modern methods in circulation include the necessary precautions but, unfortunately, many pre-1958 publications are still used, and countless recipes and methods from our grandparents' day are still current. Indeed, even in these enlightened times, a few magazines still pump out these antiquities. Their editors, always on the lookout for simple methods for their readers, refuse to believe that modern methods can turn out wines superior to many with long names and expensive pedigrees from the Continent. So the poor reader has little chance of success. Anybody with the right kind of recipe, using the right method and having a little background knowledge, can turn out wines comparable with those from almost any country you care to name. And almost the whole of the secret of success lies in preventing wines from being spoiled.

Any method that calls for gathering the fruits and then letting them ferment without added yeast should be put on the fire at once. And so should any that do not call for sterilizing the fruit either by boiling or by using sulphite (Campden

(36)

tablets), whether added yeast is recommended or not. This is because the gathered fruits already have yeasts in them. Some of them may be quite useful, but with them almost invariably come many wild (uncultivated) spoilage yeasts.

In addition to the wild yeasts, several species of bacteria and moulds are also present. If the must is not sterilized by one means or another, any of these can set up a fermentation of sorts alongside the fermentation brought about by the desirable yeast we add, so that any of the troubles mentioned above can occur very readily.

Acetification, or wine turning to vinegar, is one of the most common troubles. Although it is possible to halt this disease in its stride if detected very early, it is rare that the trouble is discovered until irreparable damage has been done. Acetification is caused by the vinegar bacteria, *Mycoderma aceti*. Having gained access to the wine or having been present on damaged fruit, the bacteria convert the alcohol produced into acetic acid which is the main constituent of vinegar.

Lactic acid bacteria, of which there are many species, are the cause of many troubles, including ropiness or oiliness. Wines afflicted with this disease take on an oily appearance and may indeed pour like oil. The flavour is impaired, but not to a great extent. However, the conditions and the appearance of the wine make it quite unpalatable.

You can cure this trouble by dissolving one and a half to two Campden tablets in each 5 l (1 gall) of wine and stirring it vigorously for several minutes. If you leave the wine for some time, the deposit settles out in a similar way to an ordinary deposit, but this one is usually of loose consistency and is easily disturbed. Some people seem content to drink a wine revived in this fashion, but to my mind the disease and the drastic treatment it requires renders a wine not worth having.

Sweet to semi-sweet wines are sometimes attacked by a species of lactic bacteria which feeds upon the sugar to produce a number of by-products which impart a peculiar off flavour, bitterness, or a very difficult to describe sickly sweetness to the wine.

This is not the same as an over-sweet wine; the sweetness appears in the after-taste rather than on the tongue. Often with these wines there are also other flavours which cannot be described as there are so many of them. And a most surprising fact is that I have had this sort of affected wine offered me at various places (no names, no pack drill) by people who simply could not detect their presence. Obviously, the disease was in its early stages, but within a few days the wine would be irretrievably lost.

Finished dry wines are not affected by lactic bacteria because of the absence of sugar. But careless production could allow the trouble to run alongside fermentation before all the sugar is used up.

In certain cases wines affected by lactic acid bacteria appear to take on a silky sheen, the density of which depends on the extent to which the disease has progressed, and this depends on the amount of sugar either attacked during fermentation or the amount of sugar left in the wine and attacked at a later stage.

Mild attacks are not easy to distinguish, but moderate to severe attacks can be seen as a silky sheen in the wine. While the disease can be cured the effects on the taste and bouquet of the wine cannot, so the only remedy for such wine is to get rid of it and thoroughly sterilize all utensils and corks that have come into contact with it.

Flowers of wine are another affliction. This is seen as tiny white flecks of mould on the surface. These gradually enlarge and join up so that the wine appears to have grown a carpet of felt. This disease is caused by mould yeast and film yeasts which attack the alcohol, converting it to carbon dioxide and water.

A cure for flowers of wine, if taken in the early stage, is to insert a tube with a funnel attached into the wine and pour similar wine into the funnel. The end of the tube should be mid-way down the jar. As the jar fills up and overflows, the mould-like flecks get expelled from the jar. Treatment thereafter is the same as that recommended for ropiness. After treatment the wine should be allowed time to clarify, then siphoned off from any deposit and used as soon as possible, because it is likely that further attacks may occur in a wine once it has been affected.

There are other causes of spoiled wines which have nothing to do with bacteria or undesirable yeasts. These come in various forms from using unsuitable utensils. Bear in mind that many utensils are quite dangerous. Those old crocks so fashionable twenty years ago and, alas, still in use in many areas, are often lead-glazed. Reaction of fruit acids on the lead can produce wines capable of giving their maker lead-poisoning. Indeed, this has happened many, many times. The cumulative effect of this is fatal.

The difference between salt-glaze, which is quite safe, and lead-glaze is usually distinguishable only by an expert. So do use modern utensils that can be trusted. In any case, a lead-glazed vessel might have hairline cracks that go unnoticed or small patches where the glaze is so thin that porous patches of clay show through. All these are hideouts for bacteria, which are unlikely to be destroyed by a quick rinse with sterilizing solution. If this sort of fault exists, then all precautions taken in other directions are wasted.

Copper, iron, zinc and what are commonly known as galvanized vessels should be avoided like the plague. There is no need to use them today, although there was little else available twenty years ago. Metal contamination, as we call it, is responsible for hazes that appear in wines at later stages. They are rarely seen until the wine has been stored and then brought out for use. Ordinary clarifiers have little or no effect on these hazes, and you usually have to resort to filtering. This can very easily cause oxidation, or the absorption of too much oxygen.

Metals, in addition to causing hazes, impart disagreeable flavours; many wines do, indeed, take on a medicinal flavour. When drinking the wine, you may think that you are taking some sort of iron tonic instead. You can rid the wines of their hazes but the flavours persist.

Sterilizing

There is no doubt that in the past – and in the present also where negligence is encountered – almost all spoilage of wines was caused by not sterilizing the initial must or utensils. Sterilizing the must is included in any good method, so there is no need to mention it here.

However, sterilization of the must is useless in preventing spoilage if we neglect to sterilize all the utensils, including bottles, corks, hydrometers and their flasks, fermenting vessels, jars and funnels. This is because the diseases which attack wines are everywhere, in the same way as those that attack humans.

Wine, like the human body, is very susceptible to attacks by bacteria. But, unlike the human body, wine has no natural means of combating attacks. In other words, there are no antibodies present in wines capable of fighting disease as there are in the human body. Every utensil must be regarded as a likely source of infection by one of the many diseases of wines. They must be sterilized in a similar fashion to the instruments used for surgical operations on the human body.

Fortunately, this is a very simple matter, which fits into the general plan of wine-making without inconvenience of any sort. To be able to do this with a minimum of bother, and to have plenty of sterilizing solution always on hand in case unexpected bottling or racking become necessary at short notice, it is important to have a stock of sulphur dioxide solution. Sulphur dioxide is undoubtedly the most reliable means of sterilization and is used by the trade. Indeed, cellars where wines are bottled are fumigated with sulphur.

Bear in mind that the many bacteria that cause disease in wine are in the air and therefore likely to be inside jars and bottles, on corks and so on. And it is a fact that many people are careless in their wine-making to the extent that they actually attract the disease to their products. Fermenting musts left uncovered, small amounts of wine or lees left in bottles or jars, fruit pulps from the straining bag, and vessels put away without being cleaned of all traces of wine – all these attract disease.

Put the pulp from a strained must outside the back door and within a few minutes there will be at least a dozen fruit flies buzzing around it. These are harmless in themselves, but they act as carriers for other diseases, especially the disease caused by acetic bacteria which convert alcohol to vinegar. For this reason, these flies are wrongly called 'vinegar flies'. Attract these flies near to the house and in minutes they will be inside if they smell wines. And if you happen to be performing some operation that necessitates exposing wines to the air for a little while, they will be after the wine like a shot.

The same applies to other bacteria. The spores of wild or spoilage yeasts and moulds are always present and are often seen in colonies as white or grey patches on jams or cheeses left exposed, on jars of meat paste, and in dirty wine and beer bottles. This being the case, yeasts and moulds must also be present on utensils, corks and so on. Though inactive they are ready to become active as soon as a medium suitable for them comes into contact with the utensils. Wine, of course, is a very suitable medium. Destruction of all these likely causes of disease is clearly necessary if trouble is to be avoided.

Sulphur dioxide is a gas. We can produce it in aqueous solution, and therefore in a very convenient form to use, by dissolving metabisulphite crystals in water. Small amounts of solution may be produced in an emergency from Campden fruit-preserving tablets used for sterilizing fruit musts, but this method is not suitable for use with a large amount of utensils or even for repeated use on small amounts. It is far better and cheaper to make a stock solution.

I find 2½ l (½ gall) of solution a very convenient amount, but half this amount would be more suitable for many people. To make 2½ l (½ gall), buy 100 g (4 oz) of sodium or potassium metabisulphite crystals from a chemist. Do not accept this if it is lumpy as it is very difficult to break down. Dissolve the crystals in about 1 litre (1¾ pt) of warm water, stirring with something non-metal such as wooden spoon, until all the crystals have dissolved. Then make up to 2½ l (½ gall) with cold water. To make the smaller amount, halve the quantities.

Corked well, the solution will keep its potency for as long as six months. It has rather a suffocating smell. However the only means of testing whether it is still strong enough after long storage and repeated use is to smell it. Do not take a powerful sniff at close quarters or at the neck of the jar. Approach it carefully, taking repeated sniffs as you get closer. All the time there is a strong smell of sulphur, the solution is suitable for use. Being so cheap, there is no excuse for using the solution once it has lost its power.

When sterilizing bottles, jars and so on, put about 1.5 dl (¼ pt) of solution into the first bottle or about 6 dl to a 5 l jar (1 pt per 1 gall jar), and shake the bottle (or jar) well so that all the inside is wetted. Then pour the solution into the next bottle, and so on until all have been treated. After you have finished, return the solution to the bulk for further use. Treat bottles and jars as they are required for use, and use them as soon as they have been treated. Before putting wine into them, drain them of solution and rinse them inside with a little, cool, boiled water.

Sulphite solution is intended mainly for use with vessels and utensils that cannot be boiled, such as glass and plastic. But it is also useful for other things as well. Straining cloths, for example, can be sterilized with it. Afterwards they should be wrung out as dry as possible and shaken well before use. Spoons and small implements, however, are best sterilized by dipping in boiling water.

When removing bungs from stored wine or removing a fermentation lock and bung, it is a wise precaution to wipe round the bung, and then the whole of the jar with a cloth well wetted with sulphite solution. This is because while the jars have been standing, dust, bacteria, yeast and mould spores will have been collecting on the surfaces. These can very easily contaminate the wine if precautions are not taken.

4
TRICKS OF THE TRADE

Racking and 'Off' Flavours

Racking is the term used to describe decanting, or removing wines from deposits that gradually build up during fermentation. These deposits are made up of minute particles of fruit (or vegetable where roots are employed) and dead yeast cells.

During the early stages of fermentation a great deal of new yeast is made and a great deal of unwanted fruit pulp with this yeast settles to the bottom of the vessel. A little of both, however, are kept in suspension by the agitation caused by the upsurge of carbon dioxide bubbles. The heavier solids forming the lees at this stage are too heavy to be kept in suspension.

Lying at the bottom, the fruit particles and yeast cells are subject to autolysis after a time. This is caused by what we might call 'further enzyme action'. (We have seen under the section on fermentation that enzymes play an important part in this process.)

It is at this stage, when much of the yeast is dead and when there is a deposit of particles of vegetable matter, that further enzyme action causes decomposition of both. And as you know anything decomposing is likely to give off smells. In the case of wines this decomposing matter is undoubtedly the cause of the development of what we call 'off' flavours. Difficult as these are to describe, you can detect them at once when you taste the wine. To avoid this unpleasant occurrence, periodic racking is desirable. But unnecessary disturbance should be avoided – by this, I mean racking every few weeks or so. This is quite unnecessary. Wine-makers with a good deal of experience will know almost instinctively when to rack and when to leave alone.

In the normal way, a method of making wines will include racking in the early stages of production in its scope of operations. For example, ten or fourteen days after yeast is added to the must and fermentation begun, the must is put into jars and the deposit left in the fermenting vessels. This is the first racking. Thereafter the wine is allowed to carry on fermenting under fermentation locks, and new deposits build up.

The need to remove this second deposit is not so urgent simply because, when the first racking took place, almost all vegetable matter was removed and a much smaller yeast colony was left to carry on the ferment. And this is why fermentation is far slower than during the early stages.

In the normal way, further racking should not be carried out for eight to ten weeks, unless a heavier-than-average deposit is building up. Normally, the yeast is not coloured by the fruit being used. So if you find that you have a deposit building up quickly and that this is coloured, it means that you have a good deal of fruit particles in the deposit. So do not delay removal of these longer than is necessary.

Racking in this fashion assists clarification. But racking should not be mistakenly used as a means of clarifying. Bear in mind that wines will not clear while there is still fermentation going on. Admittedly, I have had wines as brilliantly clear as they will ever become with occasional gas bubbles rising lazily to the surface. But there will always be exceptions to the rule, as experienced wine-makers will know.

As fermentation slows down over a period of time, the deposit likely to build up will be slight indeed. The initial racking will rid the must of the more troublesome deposits, and the second racking will take care of any remaining deposits that may cause trouble. Thereafter the build-up should be very slight and this need not be cause for alarm.

Whether or not to rack to remove this fine deposit when the wine is put away to finish clearing at the cessation of fermentation depends to a great extent on the clarity of the wine. If the wine is near-brilliant, there should be no need to rack at this stage because it will only be a matter of weeks (or even days) before the last of the minute solids in suspension have finally settled out. Then, and only then, should the wine be racked into storage jars, free from all deposit. This operation should be done by siphoning (see p. 47).

If however, there are 5 mm or so (¼ in) of deposit and the wine is still cloudy when fermentation has ceased, it would be wise to rack before putting the wine away to clear. This is advisable in case the wine takes longer than usual to become brilliant, in which event the wine would be left on the deposit longer than is desirable.

When brilliant wine is put away for storing, it is generally thought that no more deposits will form. Unfortunately, this is not the case, very often – indeed, more-often than not – wines will throw deposits even though they were brilliant to the eye when put away. When the wine is in stone jars or barrels it is impossible to tell whether further deposits have occurred because we cannot see through these as we can see through glass.

It is therefore a good plan when storing wines in stone jars or barrels to fill a bottle with the wine to be stored and cork and seal it as if it were the finished product. Label it so that you know which bulk lot it belongs to and then, after three or four months, examine the bottom of the bottle carefully. If there are deposits there, however slight, there will be slightly heavier deposits in the bulk lot. This will be evidence of the need to rack.

Sometimes, with very dark glass bottles, it is difficult to detect whether there is a deposit or not. If this problem arises, hold the wine up to the bright light and twist the bottle sharply. If a deposit is present, it will rise up into the wine like a cloud of smoke. This will settle in an hour or so.

Sweet wines, it must be understood, are often slower to clear than others, especially the very sweet ones. This is because the sugar present is in more or less the form of syrup and this, naturally, tends to slow down the settling out of the almost weightless solids.

You will appreciate that after each racking there is certain to be a little less wine. It is therefore advisable to put the wine into smaller containers each time, even if this means using 2½ l (½ gall) jars rather than larger vessels. This will mean that the advantages of bulk storing are lost. But the alternative is to store the wine with a large air-space above it. Since this air-space can lead to bacterial infection I know which alternative I prefer. Hence my recommendations in my other works and magazine articles (where I gave recipes for making 5 l (1 gall) lots) to put half in a 2½ l (½ gall) jar and bottle the remainder. This almost inevitable ending to my magazine recipes is a bit of a stock joke among the knowledgeable wine-makers. But they do agree that it is better than storing with a large air-space above the wine.

Many wine-makers anxious to store in bulk for as long as possible prefer to make more than 5 l (1 gall), say a quarter as much again as is actually required when all the processes have finished. This little extra is kept fermenting separately from the bulk and is used to top it up after each racking. In this way, whether it be 5 or 25 l (1 or 5 gall) that they want to set aside for storage, they may do so without having to leave an air-space overhead. This sort of thing is a trick of the trade that people think up for themselves.

Clarifying

In the normal way, wines clarify to brilliance without assistance of any sort, except periodic racking. This is because the method used, rather than the recipe or the type of ingredients, was the sort that does not allow for pectin or starch to appear in the must. These substances are the two most troublesome and most common causes of non-clarification.

As we have just seen, the larger particles of fruit pulp and the heavier yeast particles settle out in the early stages to form the initial heavy deposit. Even the lighter solids will settle out when the upsurge of carbon dioxide gas produced during fermentation ceases. Later, the almost weightless solids settle out. They are too light to settle out by themselves, but eventually they join up to form heavier particles and fall to the bottom of the jar. Thus wines made by methods that do not allow the presence of pectin or starch in the must will not present a clarifying problem.

When starch or pectin are present, they form a barrier which prevents the almost weightless solids from joining up to become heavier. In this way they prevent the solids from settling out. The problem is increased by the fact that the clarifiers used to clear wines not affected by starch or pectin will have no effect on these two substances except, in certain cases, to worsen matters.

The presence of pectin in a wine is almost certainly due to a faulty method of production. Pectin is found in all fruits in varying quantities. Heating the fruit releases acid which, in turn, releases the pectin. This is why the sulphiting process for fruit is so popular: it does not involve such problems. Wines produced by this method have the flavour of the raw fruit, which is most popular. But those who like wines with a stewed fruit flavour will use the pectin-destroying enzyme included in the methods to ensure a brilliantly clear wine.

Thus the sulphiting method on p. 99 and the boiling method on p. 90 will make distinctly different types of wines from the same ingredients.

Roots, of course, are a different matter. Potatoes, parsnips and carrots must be boiled in order to destroy soil bacteria. If we did nothing about this it would cloud the wine heavily in the same way as pectin, but we use a starch-destroying enzyme as included in the methods to ensure a brilliant wine. This enzyme is known as fungal amylase. If, however, you already happen to have some wine in store that is cloudy a simple test can be carried out to find whether pectin or starch is causing the trouble.

Pectin test   Take about 3 tbs (1 fl oz) of the wine and add three to four times the amount of methylated spirits. Shake well. If much pectin is present, jelly-like clots or strings will form almost immediately. If little pectin is present, some jellying will occur after about an hour. So keep the sample for a while if immediate clotting does not take place. If pectin is causing the trouble, a pectin-destroying enzyme must be employed; nothing else will do. When the pectin has been destroyed, the solids causing the clouding will join up and settle out.

Any of the pectin-destroying enzymes such as Pektolase – often call 'pectin enzymes' – are excellent and should be used according to the directions of the supplier (see list at the end of this book).

(45)

Starch test   As I mentioned before, starving the yeast of sugar in the early stages will often induce an enzyme in the yeast to convert starch to sugar. But this does not always happen so that starch causes the same kind of trouble as pectin. Root wines and those made with grains or apples are the offenders here.

To test for the presence of starch, take 2 or 3 tbs (about 1 fl oz) of the wine and add a few drops of tincture of iodine. The sample will turn dark blue or near black if starch is causing cloudiness in the wine. To test this reaction before using wine, you can see the effect if you drop a tiny amount of iodine on a slice of potato. If starch is causing the cloudiness use a starch-destroying enzyme as directed by the supplier (see list at the end of this book). This takes care of the major problems which, as we have seen, should not arise if reliable methods are used. But what of hazes caused by neither pectin or starch? There are many proprietory clarifiers which will take care of these, and it would not be fair for me to recommend one against the other. All are reliable and all are supplied with directions for use.

However, if you want to try something quite handy, then egg-white should prove satisfactory. Up to 40 l (8 gall) can be cleared with one egg-white. When using this it is best to put the wine in an open vessel, such as a fermentation vessel. Whisk the white of an egg to a stiff froth and mix it thoroughly with the wine. Return the wine to its jar. After clarification has taken place, rack in the normal way.

Filtering

I am amazed at the number of people who filter their wines almost as a matter of course, without even waiting to see whether they have a clearing problem or not. So let me say filtering should not be necessary and will not improve the flavour of any wine. Nor will it remove cloudiness caused by the presence of pectin or starch.

The main drawback with filtering is that it very often causes over-oxidation. This is caused by long exposure to oxygen in the air, which the wine absorbs. A fully robust wine may lose much of its flavour after filtering. However, delicate wines or those with, let's call them, 'tender' flavours, are likely to become quite flat and lifeless after filtering. They end up with none of the characteristics normally found in a wine. Beer is affected similarly. That occasional flat pint served over the bar is more often than not caused by oxidation.

There are modern means of avoiding this sort of thing, mainly by using various types of filters which have recently become available to home wine-makers. But this means a lot of expense for what is usually a very small quantity of wine, and I am the last person to advise unnecessary expense. For better to avoid the causes that make filtering necessary. I appreciate that most commercial wines are filtered, but commercial producers treating perhaps a thousand gallons at a time use high speed apparatus which precludes the possibility of oxidation.

Siphoning and Bottling

This is a very simple means of drawing wine from one container to another without disturbing the deposit, as would most certainly happen if the wine was poured instead. Many people shirk this operation because they think that there is some sort of mystery to it. There is no mystery, although it does fascinate many how the wine continues to flow. But what bothers many people is that they somehow break the siphon (stop the flow) and then clumsily stir up the deposit in getting it going again, thereby defeating the whole purpose of the operation.

Without siphoning wines from deposits, there would be no means of obtaining more than 2½ l clear wine from a 5 l jar (½ gall per gall). This would mean that the rest would have to be put into a suitably sized jar and allowed to clear. Even then you would be able to pour only about half of it before the sediment started to come over. Siphoning is infinitely more satisfactory because you are able to remove all but 5 mm or so (¼ in) of wine from a jar without disturbing the deposit in any way.

Where most people go wrong when siphoning is that they forget that the tops of the bottles or jar to be filled must be on a lower level than the bottom of the jar to be emptied. It is best then to put the full jar on a table and the empties on the floor or a stool.

If the jar to be emptied is on the same level as the empties, nothing would happen and if the tops of the empties were half way up the level of the full jar the full jar would only half empty because the levels become equal.

Proper siphon pumps may be had at a price. These incorporate a squeeze bulb to start the flow, but I have found that the tubing used in these is of too large a bore and that it always rests in the wine above the deposit. Such an arrangement can be regulated so that the tube goes no nearer than 2.5 cm (1 in) or so above the deposit. But the tube is so wide a bore and the suction is therefore so great that deposits are often drawn over, thereby defeating the whole purpose of the operation. By all means arrange the tube 5 cm (2 in) above the deposit, but it means that you must leave 5 cm (2 in) of wine behind.

So the best plan is to make a siphon arrangement for yourself. Wine supply shops stock your needs. And these merely consist of a length of glass tubing with the last 2.5 cm (1 in) of one end turned up and a metre or so of non-toxic clear polythene tubing. An additional item is a small ebonite tap to fit to the other end of the tube. Now all you have to do is to take one end of the polythene tubing, immerse about 5 cm (2 in) of one end in hot water for a minute or two and then while it is hot manipulate it over the straight end of the glass tube so

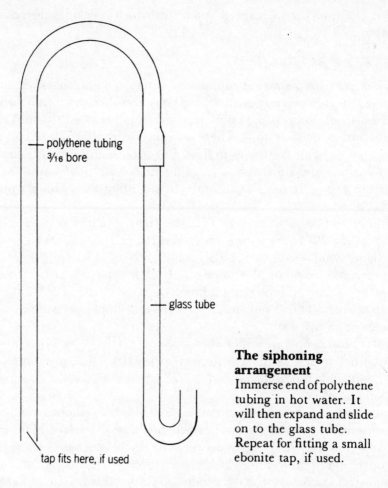

polythene tubing
³⁄₁₆ bore

glass tube

tap fits here, if used

The siphoning arrangement
Immerse end of polythene tubing in hot water. It will then expand and slide on to the glass tube. Repeat for fitting a small ebonite tap, if used.

that about 2.5 cm (1 in) goes on. As it cools it takes on a mighty grip and will not slide off. The little tap, if you can get one, is fitted to the other end of the polythene tubing and your siphon is complete. If you cannot buy a tap as shown in the illustration you can do without it.

With this arrangement, all you have to do is to put the full jar of wine on a table and the bottles on the floor or a stool. Lower the upturned end of the glass tubing carefully into the jar so that it comes to rest against the bottom inside edge with the U bend resting on the bottom of the jar. You will see that the open end of the glass tube is above the deposit, and because the suction will not be above, as would be the case with a tube hovering over the deposit, the deposit cannot be drawn into the tube, unless you disturb it by stirring it up accidentally. The next step is to hold the tube firmly at the neck of the jar, take the other end of the plastic tube, whether a tap is fitted or not, and suck it gently until the

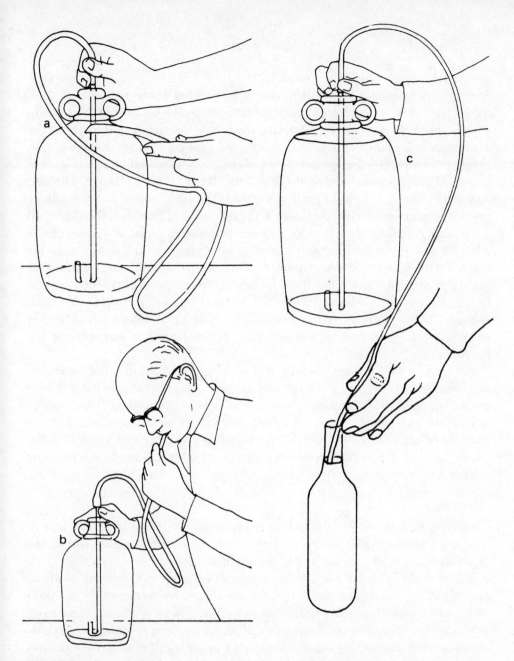

The siphoning method

a Lower glass tube to bottom of jar of wine so that the curved end of the tube rests on the bottom of the jar. The open end remains above the deposit.

b Suck the other end of the polythene tubing until the wine reaches your lips.

c Close the tap or pinch the tubing, lower it into the awaiting empty bottle (the top of which must be lower than the bottom of the jar to be emptied), and allow the wine to flow. Fill the bottle to $^1/_3$ way into the neck. When the bottle is full enough, pinch tubing or close tap and transfer to next bottle.

(49)

wine reaches your lips. When this happens, pinch the tube tightly to stop the flow (or turn off the tap), lower this end in the first bottle and let the wine flow. As the bottle fills into the neck, squeeze the tube to slow up the flow. When the wine is one-third way into the neck stop the flow altogether, put the tube in the next bottle and allow the wine to flow again. As the jar empties to quarter full, slowly tilt it towards the upturned end of the glass tube so that all the wine is drawn off, being careful to stop the flow if the deposit begins to move. The best way to do this is to return the jar to upright so that the upturned end rises above the last centimetre of wine. Actually, if the deposit is as firm as it should be, all but a small glassful of wine should be drawn over. If you are new to siphoning, it might be wise to get a second pair of hands to hold the tube at the neck of the jar and to tilt the jar when it is nearly empty. Do bear in mind that you will need six standard British wine bottles, or seven (perhaps eight) long-necked shoulderless-type continental wine bottles to 5 l (1 gall) of wine. So have enough bottles ready in position and have your corks ready too. There is nothing worse than finding you are short of something at this stage of the operation.

When you have finished bottling and corking your wine fit a plastic seal to each as shown on p. 18. Then use one of the many attractive labels available today, but do write on the label before you stick it on the bottle. All you need to write is the name of the wine, the month and year of making and whether it is sweet, medium or dry. If it is fortified with spirit you can put a small 'F' in the corner or a 'P' if it is preserved with Campden tablets. This is just for your reference.

Correcting Faults

Correcting or adjusting faults in finished wines is all part of the know-how of wine-making, and herein lie many of the tricks of the trade together with many of the skills that go to make a clever wine-maker.

When making wines we set out to produce a certain type of product. Sometimes we succeed so easily that we are almost embarrassed by our good fortune. At other times obtaining what we really want calls for some skill. Whatever our aim, we can obtain it, or get as near to it as is humanly possible, without much trouble, provided that we have a rough idea of what we want and how to set about getting it.

In the first place we use a recipe and method that will produce what we are after. But it sometimes happens that the end product is not quite what we wanted. There may be too much acid present, or the wine may be either too sweet or too dry. These are not really faults as such, because whatever sort of wine you get, some will acclaim it the finest they have tasted while others will shudder at it. It is all a matter of taste, and surely the skill in making wines comes in making the type of variety you really like. This is easy enough when you have gained experience in making a wide variety of wines, even if it means treating the finished product in some way.

Make no mistake about this, your favourite commercial product whether it be wine or whisky could not be produced without after-treatment of some sort, usually blending. In the case of the higher-alcohol wines, such as ports and sherries, fortifying is also carried out because, like us, commercial producers cannot produce more alcohol than the yeast will make. If it were not for this, commercial products would not be stronger than those made by home wine-makers.

Over-acid wines An over-acid wine will naturally show itself by making you wince. The simplest means of reducing the acid in an over-acid wine is to blend it with a similar wine which lacks acid. Lack of acid is usually noticed as lack of bite, that is, having swallowed the wine, it is gone. There is nothing left on the palate to tell you that you have, in fact, tasted wine rather than something else with a fruity flavour. Obviously the blending improves both the wines – the over-acid and the under-acid.

But how do you reduce acidity if you have no wine lacking in acid? The simplest means of correcting this is to use pure medicinal chalk (precipitated chalk) from a chemist. First, it should be decided how over-acid the wine is, and whether the fault is, in fact, over-acidity rather than harshness caused by an excess of tannin. It should be made clear, though, that young wines sometimes have a slightly acid and harsh taste as well. Therefore young wines should never be treated, but should be kept until they are a year old. By that time many of the suspected faults will have ironed themselves out. If after a year a wine is still over-acid, then treatment with chalk is justified.

Put the wine into an open vessel such as fermentation vessel, and treat a sample (say 6 dl or 1 pt). Take a little of the sample and stir in a teaspoonful of chalk, then mix this with the remainder. After treating the bulk with this doctored sample, allow the chalk to settle out until the wine is brilliant again before tasting. This method reduces the risk of taking out too much acid.

If further treatment is necessary you can do this without removing the wine from the chalk deposit. After removing the required amount of acid, allow the wine to clarify to brilliance – which will take less than an hour – and then siphon it into bottles or a jar for further storage. If by accident, you remove too much acid, add a little citric or tartaric acid to make it up.

Rough wines Rough or harsh wines usually have a rather stronger all-round flavour than is wanted, with a noticeable harshness on the palate.

Certain fruit wines made from rather more fruit than usual will produce this type of fault. Elderberry is a notable offender in this respect. So it is wise to stick to a well-tried recipe and not exceed 1.8 kg (4 lb) per 5 l (1 gall). This amount will not produce an excess of acid provided that all the fruits are ripe. Nor will this amount produce an excess of tannin provided that the pulp is not fermented for too long.

You will often find harshness in a new wine, but delay treatment for a year or so to enable self-rectification to take place if it will. Treating for roughness too soon may result in a considerable lack of desirable characteristics when a treated wine has ironed out its own faults. The overall effects can be that twice the amount of roughness has been removed when half of it should have remained to give the wine necessary character.

When roughness persists after a year of storage whisk half of the white of an egg into a froth with a little of the wine and stir it into the bulk. Allow to settle out and then taste the wine. If similar further treatment is necessary, do it before taking the wine off this first deposit. Be careful not to take out too much, although you remedy this by adding a pinch of grape tannin. Allow the treated wine to clarify to brilliance and then bottle it or put it into jars for further storage. The half of an egg-white recommended is for the experimental treatment of 5 l (1 gall). When treating larger amounts, increase the amount of egg-white accordingly.

When egg-white is added to the wine, it forms an insoluble cloud which surrounds tannin and other constituents causing the harshness and takes them to the bottom of the jar.

This treatment is necessary only with red wines, and then only rarely, but it is as well to know what to do.

Blending

As I think I have written elsewhere (I have written so much about this subject that half has been forgotten), I firmly believed in my early days that if I made wine from elderberries or blackberries then it must be from these alone, without any addition of any sort.

I felt that if I could not make a good wine from these fruits alone, I had no business making wines at all. Besides, I believed that wine must be labelled according to the fruit used. However, my early prejudice against blending has been completely knocked for six by modern arguments and practice. Blending either the ingredients or the finished wines is now common and it is very often the only means of achieving particular results.

This is not to say that top-class wines are not to be obtained from a single ingredient: they certainly are. For example, English wild and garden fruits and concentrated grape juice make top-class wines that satisfy the most educated palates without other ingredients being used. However, many ingredients do not make good wines by themselves. Take roots and flowers, for example. They must be blended with other ingredients, such as citrus fruits and dried fruits. Today all good recipes include either or both of these with the basic ingredients. The end product is what counts. Bananas too must be blended with other ingredients. To obtain special results, blending the finished wines is often the only answer. And it is very often the only means of correcting faults.

Very many wine-makers make large amounts of individual wines for the sole purpose of blending them. They make, for example, a large batch of dry wine, which is always the easiest to make. They keep, say, 5 l (1 gall) of this as dry. Then they blend the second 5 l (1 gall) of the batch with a sweet wine made with different fruit to give them a medium-sweet wine of a varied type, and blend, say, a third 5 l (1 gall) with some other wine. In this way, they know from experience that they will obtain the special results they are after which could not be produced in any other way, not even by blending the various fruits before making the wines.

Blending needs common sense and a sense of purpose. It is no use at all adding one wine to another just to see what happens. Due consideration should be given not only to what you want but also to whether the wines you are considering blending will give the results you are aiming at. Can I help you in this respect? I cannot, simply because I do not know what you are likely to want to achieve by blending.

All I can do is to tell you which wines will blend well to prevent you spoiling several good wines. On no account blend for the sake of blending as this sort of thing can lead to disappointment.

The simplest and the best way of blending is by using several glasses. For instance, take three rows of three glasses (a dilution of one in three will probably be quite enough for most blending purposes). In the first glass of each row put one teaspoonful of the first wine. In the second glass of each row put two teaspoonfuls of the first wine, and in the third, three. Then add one teaspoonful of the second wine to each glass in the first row (this will give you blends of 1: 1; 2 : 1; and 3 : 1). Add two teaspoonfuls of the second wine to each glass in the second row (this gives you 1 : 2; 2 : 2; 3 : 2). And add three teaspoonfuls of the second wine to each glass in the third row (this gives you 1 : 3; 2 : 3; 3 : 3). You can of course omit 2 : 2 and 3 : 3 which are the same as 1 : 1, but the other dilutions will give you seven blends from which to choose. Sample each blend, take a small piece of cheese between samples to clear the palate, and if you have chosen your two wines carefully in the first place, one of the blends will give you the result you are after.

When you have found it, you will know from the number of teaspoonfuls of each wine used how many bottles of each you need to make up 2½ or 5 l (½ or

1 gall). When you have done this, put the blended wine away for six months for the blends to 'marry'. This is far more important than most people imagine. Marrying or interweaving of the various constituents, bouquets, esters and so on, takes time. When this is complete, the blended wine should be of top quality.

The following groups of wines blend well with each other:

Group 1
black plum
elderberry
blackberry
damson
blackcurrant
bilberry (herts or blueberry)
mulberry
black grape (fruit or concentrate)

Usually, only two wines are needed, but three and sometimes even four may be used.

Group 2
raspberry
white grape (fruit or concentrate)
mulberry
loganberry
damson
redcurrant
whitecurrant
dried fruit wines (except elderberry and bilberry)
sloe (fresh or dried)

Group 3
rhubarb
dried fruit wines (except elderberry, sloe and bilberry)
root wines (except beetroot)

Over-sweet white fruit wines blend well with a little rhubarb. Certain wines that may be lacking in acid (but not red wines) also blend well with rhubarb.

Group 4
peach
apricot
white grape (fresh fruit or concentrate)

Flower wines rarely blend well either with themselves or with fruit wines. But a dash of rhubarb wine has been known to improve them. Some wine-makers, however, maintain that they obtain very excellent blends of flower wines. But there will always be someone to contradict me.

In any event, blending should not be resorted to for its own sake. If you have really good wines that can stand on their own feet and knock people off theirs, why try to improve them? Seriously, though, blending for the sake of it can not only irrevocably spoil really good wines but also disappoint the blender.

The same applies to blending ingredients. Once you have found a good recipe that makes the wine you like, it is wise to leave the recipe as it is. But if you really feel that the wine would have been just that much better if there had been a little more of 'this' or perhaps a little less of 'that', then there is absolutely no reason at all for not altering the blend of ingredients to suit your own taste. Or you can even add an ingredient not included in the recipe.

I have evolved hundreds of recipes by doing just this sort of thing, taking into account that one ingredient will add fruitiness, another body and some bouquet, another acid, and yet another tannin, all in suitable proportions. Judging by the popularity of my recipes, which have produced wines that have won and still do win prizes all over the country, my choice of ingredients has been reasonably good.

This is not to say that I am infallible; I have turned out some pretty disappointing wines at times. But this is how I obtained my knowledge. Any wine-maker wishing to evolve his own recipes must take account of the constituents necessary in an initial must and in a finished wine. If he does and bears in mind the types of ingredients that will put these constituents into a must, he will, with practice, evolve some excellent recipes.

5
THE HYDROMETER

*Using the Hydrometer **.

Many people go through their wine-making lives without using the hydrometer and this is quite understandable, for the truth is that it is not an essential in making good wines. But it does perform a very useful service and it is known that many people would use it if they could get to understand it. For some reason many people find it confusing and I think I can explain the reason for this.

We use a thermometer to measure temperature whether it be of air, hot liquids or our own when we are ill. But when we use a thermometer, we use nothing by way of comparison. When using the hydrometer we use water as the comparison factor, but this need not confuse anybody. Water has what we call the gravity of 1000. It has been given this figure because many liquids – especially spirits such as whisky or methylated spirits – are thinner (less dense) than water, so they, compared with water, have a gravity below 1000, and the reading would appear as 0999 or whatever it happened to be. Conversely, many liquids, especially those we prepared for wine-making, have a greater density (or are thicker) than water. Therefore compared with water, with its gravity of 1000, the liquids we prepare for wine-making have a reading above 1000; how much above this figure depends upon the amount of sugar in the mixture. And let me say at once that all we are really concerned with is the figure above the 1000. On p. 58 is an illustration of three hydrometers side by side. One is floating in pure water and shows a gravity of 1000; the other two are floating in fruit juices with differing amounts of sugar present. If you now look at the hydrometer table on p. 57 you will be able to see at once how much alcohol these two amounts of sugar will make.

Just to help you get used to reading the table the specific gravity of 1030 will make 3.6% of alcohol by volume, while the reading of 1050 will make 6.4% by volume. The difference between alcohol by volume and proof spirit is on p. 75.

*Hydrometer readings can be written in different ways: 1150, 1.150, 150 all mean effectively the same.

The Hydrometer

Hydrometer Table

Specific gravity	Potential alcohol by volume %
1020	2.4
1030	3.6
1040	4.0
1050	6.4
1060	7.7
1070	9.0
1080	10.5
1090	11.9
1100	13.4
1110	14.5
1120	16.0

'Specific gravity'. All this means is 'the gravity as compared with water'. Therefore the figures 20, 30 and so on, up to 120, in the table are all we are really concerned with.

The importance of the hydrometer in most people's minds is that it enables them to make a wine of a given percentage of alcohol and at the same time allows them to check if they have actually made it. This is most important to people making dry wines when 10% or 11% of alcohol by volume is plenty. These people of course do not add sugar as given in a recipe. They calculate that 65 g (2¼ oz) of sugar will raise the gravity by 5 on the hydrometer in one gallon of must while 130 g (5 oz) will raise the reading by 10.

They calculate how much sugar to add and then check the reading. This is done simply by filling a trial jar with some of the prepared liquid and then sliding the hydrometer into the sample, which must be standing on a level surface.

The hydrometer must float clear of all parts of the flask. The reading is taken where the liquid cuts across the stem. This then, is the specific gravity. It can be increased by adding more sugar, bearing in mind that 65 g (2 ¼ oz) will raise the reading by 5, or it can be reduced by adding water or fruit juice.

If you begin making wine with specific gravity of 1110 you should finish up with a reading of 1000 or perhaps a fraction under this, say 0999. This means that the yeast has used up all the sugar and you have a dry wine of 14.5% by volume. But as mentioned, dry wines are best for being in the region of 10% or 11% by volume so it is best to start with a specific gravity of 1080 or 1090 for dry wines, unless you want dry wines higher in alcohol. It is for you to decide.

The sweeter wines must of course be higher in alcohol, and because all the

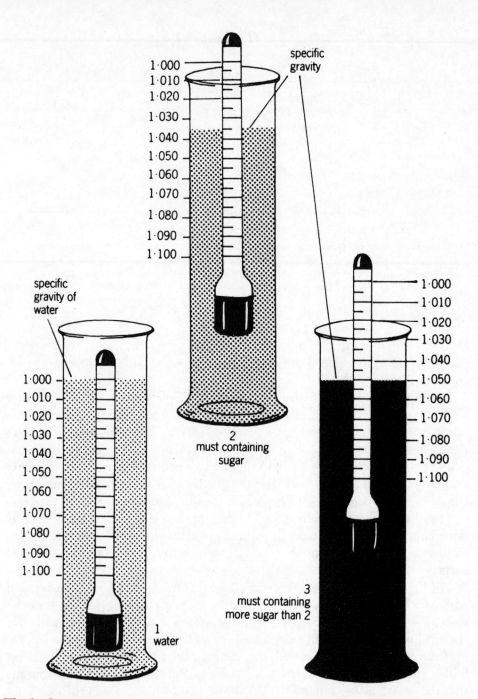

specific gravity

specific gravity of water

1·000
1·010
1·020
1·030
1·040
1·050
1·060
1·070
1·080
1·090
1·100

1·000
1·010
1·020
1·030
1·040
1·050
1·060
1·070
1·080
1·090
1·100

1·000
1·010
1·020
1·030
1·040
1·050
1·060
1·070
1·080
1·090
1·100

2
must containing sugar

1
water

3
must containing more sugar than 2

The hydrometer

In these illustrations the scale which appears on the hydrometer in the normal way has been put beside the trial jar so that the scale can be enlarged for easy reading.

Bearing in mind that 2¼ oz sugar represents 5 on the hydrometer, we can easily work out how much sugar the two sample musts in this illustration contain.

(58)

sugar up to 1110 on the hydrometer will be used up during fermentation, some sugar will have to be added for sweetening purposes. How much depends on personal tastes but on the whole 100-150 g (4-6 oz) of sugar unfermented in one gallon of wine is usually ample.

In the table on p. 57 I have quoted the figure 1120 as giving a potential alcohol content of 16% by volume. And if fermentation is as satisfactory as it should be this amount of alcohol will be made. But, and it is often a big but, this is not always the case. So it is often wise to assume that you will not make more than 15%, which is represented by a specific gravity of 1115. Indeed many people, for some reason or other, never obtain an alcohol content of above 14.5%. This is not calamitous because 14% or just over is a nice percentage that ensures that the wine will keep well.

Now let us see what happens to a must prepared as described, after fermentation has begun until it ceases. As most of you will know, fermentation may last for several weeks, or it may be over in a few weeks. In Fermentation Chart 1 (below), I have tried to give a reasonably representative picture of the progress of fermentation. But do not expect your ferments to progress in an identical fashion. This is merely an illustration of what might happen under ordinary home conditions.

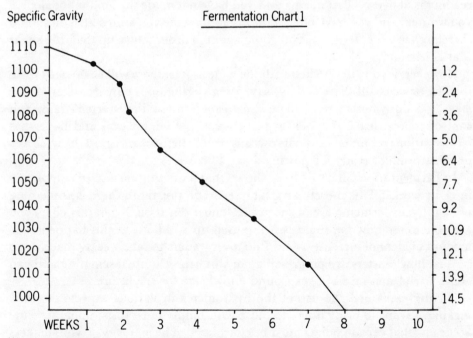

We see that figures on the left of the chart are in the reverse of their order on the hydrometer itself. This has been arranged so that you may see how, as the sugar is used up the readings drop and the alcohol content increases.

As soon as fermentation begins, there is some natural warming of the must because of yeast action. This can lead you to think that an appreciable drop in sugar content has taken place in the first day or so. What happens is this. The must expands slightly as it gets warmer, and this lowers its density and therefore a hydrometer reading, if one is taken. So do not take a reading of the must until a week after fermentation has begun. By that time the temperature of the must will be reasonably normal. If you are using a fermentation cupboard, where the temperature of the must will be around 18°C (65°F), the warming effect will not be noticeable.

In the example of fermentation I have illustrated in Fermentation Chart 1, you will see that the hydrometer reading has dropped from 1110 to 1000. This is merely representative. The fact is that the reading when all fermentation has ceased might well be below 1000. This is because all sugar has been fermented out and alcohol is now present. Alcohol is lighter than water, and therefore it could very well be that a well-fermented dry wine would have specific gravity lower than that of water. In this case your hydrometer would sink to just below the 1000 mark.

When you get a drop of 110 it means that you have made the amount of alcohol you wanted. But if you find that fermentation has stopped and that the reading is above 1000, it means that you have not made the amount of alcohol you wanted, and you have not got the bone-dry wine you aimed at. You should therefore try to get fermentation going again in order to use up the little sugar that is left.

However, if you are satisfied with the wine as it is, there will be no need to do this. In any case, if there is only, say, 5 registering on the hydrometer at this stage, I doubt whether you will be able to get fermentation started again. You can, of course, leave the lock in place, keep the wine warm and hope that fermentation recommences on its own, as it will often do, or regard the wine as a finished product ready for putting away to clear.

In Fermentation Chart 1 I have shown that fermentation ceased completely in eight weeks. This merely an example, so do not think there is something wrong if your ferments are of shorter or longer duration. From this chart you are able to see how the sugar is being used up and how, as this happens, the amount of alcohol increases. And I do urge readers to take weekly readings to see just how matters are progressing, for this can be quite fascinating and can add a useful measure of background knowledge for the future.

Having explained the use of the hydrometer in various aspects of wine-making, I want to bring home to those who simply must insist upon absolute accuracy, that certain points must be considered. The majority of wine-makers will be content to go ahead on the readings they obtain when finding the specific gravity of their musts and be quite content with the result of the fermentation and wine resulting from it. But it would be unfair if I were not to let others know that there are small factors which should be taken into account, if they insist upon accuracy.

The illustration below shows an enlarged section of the hydrometer in a sample must. In this is illustrated what we call surface tension. What we mean by this is that sugar solutions, and even water to lesser extent, tend to climb a little way up the stem of the hydrometer. The greater the sugar content, the higher is the surface tension.

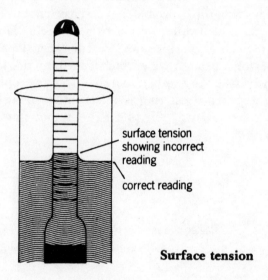

surface tension
showing incorrect
reading

correct reading

Surface tension

So when taking readings, take care to read the hydrometer strictly at eye level, and watch carefully for surface tension. Another factor is that, as most of you know already, a must is not made up merely of sugar and water. Neither are fruit juices. There are other constituents which have a small effect upon the hydrometer readings.

For example, the acids and pectin in fruits tend to increase the reading slightly. To allow for this, it is wise to regard the sugar content as being 3 lower than the reading states. This would be ample for musts containing the usual 1.5-2.5 kg of fruit to 5 l (about 4-6 lb per gall). But when, say, 3.5 kg (8 lb) or more are used and when grapes are being fermented, it would be wise to allow as much as 5 and deduct this from the reading.

Where dried fruits alone are being used, this allowance is not necessary, but if equal quantities of dried and fresh fruits are being used, half the figures quoted would be enough, depending on whether you are using ordinary English garden or wild fruits or grapes with the dried fruits.

The Hydrometer and Sweet Wines

Making sweet wines is more successful when the hydrometer is used. I say this because it is always best to start off with a specific gravity of 1110. And by using the hydrometer we are able to start with the right amount of sugar in the must. How much sugar the must contains before you add any depends on the sugar content of the fruit and the amount of fruit used. With English garden and wild fruits the amount will be very little, but it is worth knowing how much.

When making sweet wines we do exactly the same as described for dry wines to start with. We start fermentation in the normal way and watch its progress by taking readings with the hydrometer. These need not be frequent; weekly or fortnightly will do. Meanwhile, we must try to decide how much sugar left unfermented will make a wine medium sweet or sweet. This will depend a very great deal on personal taste. A wine which is medium dry to medium sweet to one person may be sweet to another, and so on. Some people like a sweet wine with only 10° of sugar left registering as unfermented on the hydrometer. As we have seen, this 10 represents 130 g (4½ oz) of sugar. But others would want more than this.

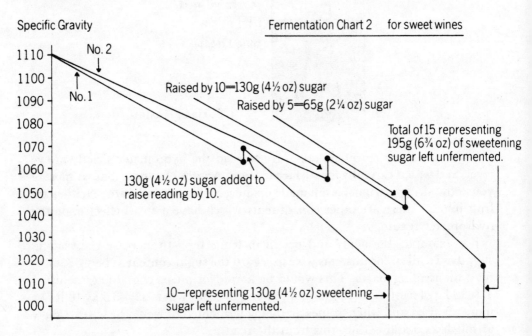

Specific Gravity

Fermentation Chart 2   for sweet wines

So it is a matter of trial and error according to personal taste how much sugar to add in addition to the amount that will be used in making the alcohol we want. So we begin the ferment with a reading of 1110 knowing that this amount of sugar will be fermented out in making the alcohol we want, and, as some sugar is used up, we add a little more. This extra will be left unfermented and will register on the hydrometer when all fermentation has ceased. In the Fermentation Chart on p. 62 you will see exactly what I mean. You will see that with ferment no. 1 we began with a reading of 1110 and when the reading dropped to 1060 we added 130 g (4½ oz) of sugar. This raised the reading from 1060 to 1070.

Now it is a fact that by adding sugar bit by bit we seem to be able to induce the yeast to make a little more alcohol than it otherwise might. But this is not something that you should count on, although it often happens. So you should always work on the assumption that you will not make more than 15% of alcohol by volume. If you do make more alcohol, and more sugar is used up in consequence, so much the better. But then you will have to add a little more sugar to give the wine the sweetness you want.

The effect of this is shown in Fermentation Chart 2 as ferment no. 2. In this we made two additions: one of 130 g (4½ oz) (10) when the reading had fallen to 1050 thereby raising it to 1060; and another of 65g (2½ oz) (5) when the reading had dropped to 1040 raising the reading to 1045. In both cases we obtain a total drop of 110.

The Hydrometer and Pulp Ferments

Pulp ferments as we call them are fruit musts fermented on the pulp, or where the fruits are crushed and the skins and pips fermented for a time.

To take an accurate reading (to obtain the correct specific gravity) you will have to crush the fruit well, and mix it with water, as in the many recipes and methods describing this type of ferment. Add the initial 900 g (2 lb) of sugar with the remainder of the water, and then take a sample of the must. Strain out the solids through several thicknesses of muslin. You only need enough liquid to fill the trial jar. You can then make any adjustment required merely by consulting the other parts of this section.

The above applies to all garden and wild fruits. Musts made from grapes only are handled a little differently. This is because they contain a great deal of sugar, so much so, in fact, that it is always best to find the specific gravity before adding any sugar at all. It is a fact that some grapes, especially in a good season, will contain enough sugar to make an excellent dry wine without adding any sugar at all. But we cannot rely on this, so we must find out the specific gravity of the juice before we begin. And here a hydrometer which reads from 1000 to 1100 will suffice. Grapes are usually used alone and the juice left undiluted. Grapes bought from a greengrocer would make the cost of wine prohibitive – though some people seem able to afford it.

At this point I can let you into a little dodge that often works; I have done it late on a Saturday evening in certain London markets. Street traders packing up for the weekend will often sell off the remainder of their grapes at much less than the quoted price because they know that by the Monday – a day on which there is little demand for such fruit – the grapes will be past their best and by the Tuesday quite unsaleable. I have bought boxes of Cape grapes containing more than 14 lb, marked up at 50p a pound, for as little as £2.00. But you will have to bargain with them; otherwise they will diddle you with a smile and a conscience as clear as brilliant wine.

It is impossible to say with any certainty how many grapes are required to make 5 l (1 gall) of wine. This is because the juice content will vary with each sort. This is dealt with elsewhere in this book. All we are concerned with in this section is finding the specific gravity of the juice of the grapes.

The first thing to do, therefore, is to crush them well by hand and wring them out by the handful in order to get all the sugar into the juice. The fact that the pulp is not strained from the juice does not matter. When the grapes are thoroughly crushed, take a small sample of the juice and strain it through several thicknesses of muslin. Put this into the hydrometer jar, and take the reading as for other juices.

You are then able to work out how much sugar you need to add to bring the specific gravity up to 1110 (or 1100 if this suits you), simply by looking up the details for other wines in this chapter. If you want to make sweet wines from grapes, you will tell at once by reading the appropriate section how adding sugar during fermentation affects the readings, and how to calculate how much sugar is being used and the amount of alcohol you have made when all fermentation has ceased.

The Hydrometer and Concentrated Grape Juices

When using the Hidalgo range of concentrated grape juices (see address at the end of this book) there is no need to use the hydrometer unless you want to. This is because the cans they are supplied in hold 1.2 l (2 pt) which make 5 l (1 gall) of wine, or a 2.4 l (4 pt) which make 10 l (2 gall), or 5 l (4 gall) which makes 20 l (4 gall); and all have a specific gravity of 1400. When we make 1.2 l into 5 l (2 pt into 1 gall), or the larger sizes into 10 or 20 l (2 or 4 gall), we reduce the figure 400 to 100. This is because we have made the original amount into four times as much. When we dilute as we do, it must be borne in mind that all we are concerned with is the figure above the 1000. This is because it represents the sugar content, while the figure 1000 only refers to the water. To make it abundantly clear we have:

water	1000
Sugar	100
Specific gravity of diluted juice	1100

As will be seen from the hydrometer table on p. 57 this reading will produce a wine of roughly 12% of alcohol by volume and the wine will be dry. If you want more alcohol than this you will have to add sugar to give a reading of 1110. In other words, raise the gravity by 10 on the hydrometer. As we have seen, 65 g (2¼ oz) of sugar will raise the reading by 5. So to achieve the maximum alcohol all that need be done is to add 130 g (4½ oz) of sugar and this is best done by dissolving it in some of the water to be used for diluting the concentrate. Just warm a little of this, dissolve the sugar in it, stir it into the concentrate and then make the whole up to 5 l (1 gall). The above example refers to making 1.2 l into 5 l (2 pt into 1 gall). If you were making 2.4 l into 10 l (4 pt into 1 gall) you would need 260 g (9 oz) of sugar, or 520 g (18 oz) if you were making 5 l into 20 l (1 gall into 4 galls). When you have added the sugar to give the maximum alcohol the wine will still be dry. So if you want a sweet wine you will have to add a little more so that it remains unfermented. Generally all that is needed in 5 l (1 gall) is an additional 50 g (2 oz) for a medium and 100 g (4 oz) for a fully sweet wine, but much depends on personal tastes.

So much for the Hidalgo range. However, there is a very wide range of other excellent concentrates on the market and most of these come in cans or sachets containing 1 kg (2 lb 3 oz or 27 fl oz) as against the 1.2 l (40 fl oz or 2 pt) of the Hidalgo range. I have found that when one of these is diluted to make 5 l (1 gall) of wine the specific gravity is only around 1060, to give an alcohol content of around 7.7% by volume which is only just enough for a low alcohol dry wine. But this is not necessarily the case with all the concentrates available. Since it is important both for deciding how much alcohol you want your wine to contain and whether you want a dry, medium or sweet wine, you will have to use the hydrometer to find the specific gravity when one of these cans has been made into 5 l (1 gall) of must with water. My method for making wines from concentrated grape juices is quite simple. The directions on some of the cans make it all so complicated and involved that I devised the following simple method for all the concentrates.

My method with concentrated grape juice   It very often happens that when concentrates have been standing for some time the sugar settles to the bottom of the can and becomes quite solid. So the first thing to do is to wipe the top of the can clean with a damp cloth, then open it and stand it in hot water over gentle heat, stirring occasionally. In a few minutes the juice will be ready to pour into the fermenting pail. When you have done this, make up to 5 l (1 gall) with boiled water that has cooled. Make sure all the sugar is dissolved and that the concentrate is mixed thoroughly with the water, otherwise you will obtain an inaccurate hydrometer reading. When you are ready, take a sample of the mixture into your trial flask, stand it on a level surface and gently slide the

(65)

hydrometer into it. The hydrometer must float clear of all parts of the flask – in other words it must not touch the bottom or sides. Add more juice to the flask if the hydrometer touches bottom. As the hydrometer floats, take the reading where the juice cuts across the stem and compare this with the figures given in the hydrometer table on p. 57.

From this you will see how much you need to raise the gravity to whatever alcohol content you wish. Bear in mind that all the sugar will be fermented out with a starting reading of 1110 or less, so all the wines made with this reading or below this will be dry.

Having decided how much you have to raise the gravity, bear in mind that 65 g (2¼ oz) of sugar will raise the reading by 5 and work out how much sugar you need to add. This will have to be dissolved in some of the diluted concentrate, so put the sugar in a pyrex or polythene jug, pour over it some of the mixture, stand the jug in a saucepan of hot water over gentle heat and stir until the sugar is dissolved. Then pour this into the mixture, add the yeast and continue as for any other wine.

Note that you do not use additional water to dissolve the sugar otherwise you will not get the type of wine you intend. And do not take an hydrometer reading after adding the sugar; you will not get the exact figure you aimed at because the sugar will have increased the overall volume of the liquid to some extent. For example 900 g (2 lb) of sugar occupies the space of 6 dl (1 pt), and if you try to rectify matters you will be at it for hours on end because each small sugar addition will increase the overall volume of the liquid. So when you have added the sugar to give you the reading you want, leave it at that.

6
THE LAST STAGES

Maturing

There is no doubt that maturing is the final phase in the production of quality wines. And, alas, it is true that a multitude of amateur wine-makers never let their wines prove themselves. Many of them think: 'This wine tastes all right as it is, I can't see it improving all that much. So here goes.' And, hey presto, it has gone almost before the next batch is in the fermenting vessel. But if they would put away even one bottle and taste it in a year or two, how they would kick themselves for drinking the rest so young.

Such vast differences are found between young and old wines that it is not unrealistic to liken young wines to boisterous, ill-mannered children and old wines to gentle old folk with loveable dispositions. Despite this, young wines are often quite good and worth drinking as they are, but they improve gradually over a couple of years. Generally young wines are quite rough and sharp to the palate with nothing really to recommend them other than promise of better things to come. Some, in fact, are so 'disappointing' that I have known people to think that they have gone wrong in one way or another.

When, years ago, we formed a wine-making circle in the area in which I live, one member actually brought a gallon along to ask my opinion. It had ceased fermenting a few weeks earlier. It was quite brilliant, but was rough and lacked bouquet. Although the flavour was not as good as it should have been for the type of wine, I knew that all it needed was a couple of years to settle down. I could not really find fault with such young wine. When I told this member to keep it for a couple of years because it would improve beyond all recognition he, like most disbelieving beginners, simply would not be conviced. He would have none of it, thinking as many do that I was just kidding him. Honestly, I often wonder whether people like that want to learn or not.

Anyway, he told me that he wanted the jar for another batch and, if I liked it, I could take it and let him have the jar at the next meeting. This I did because I

(67)

knew it was useless to argue with one who had already made up his mind. It was about two years later when I took along a bottle as my sample for the evening. The member who gave me that gallon was there as usual. When his turn came to taste my wine he went into raptures over it, even offering to buy a couple of bottles for Christmas if I had them to spare. I had to confess that I had only five bottles because he had given me a gallon! He was dumbfounded.

All young wines must be given time to develop, except perhaps the very driest, which rarely improve after a year unless they are very rough. Others really ought to be given two years at least. I realize that this is a very long time for those anxious to drink their wines because they have nothing to drink for two or three years from the time they start out. The easiest way out of this problem is to make a large amount of suitable varieties and, while some can be drunk young, the larger part of each batch can be allowed to mature. In this way, although you will be drinking immature and therefore inferior wines, you will at least have something while the rest is improving.

How to store the maturing wines is a matter not very easily solved because most amateurs rarely make sufficient of the one sort to fill a barrel. But those who do make amounts of 25 and 50 l (5 and 10 gall) really ought to consider storing them in 22½ or 45 l (4½ or 9 gall) barrels.

It is during storage in wooden containers of this sort that oxygen percolates through the pores of the wood in very tiny beneficial amounts to cause much desired oxidation. This, it must be understood, is certainly different to the over-oxidation that can take place when the whole of the wine is exposed to air, say, when filtering.

When in barrels, chemical changes and reactions are constantly taking place. Some run with each other, or concurrently, while others depend on the one before, and therefore run consecutively. All that takes place is very far from being understood. But we do know that maturing really means the marrying, or shall we call it the interweaving, of the many constituents that go to make up a wine.

Flavours are improved by chemical action, while esters develop to produce a bouquet. But these processes would be interrupted and the result hindered if unnecessary racking or other disturbances were allowed. Therefore, wines put away in bulk should not be disturbed – not even moved from one place to another – if it is at all possible to avoid doing so.

Time is the important factor because maturing should always be slow. In fact, you are unlikely to be able to hurry it. Deciding just when a wine is mature is probably the hardest part of wine-making. And I doubt whether anybody could hope to decide for you when wines have matured sufficiently in bulk to be bottled to finish maturing. This is something peculiar to each wine, probably because each contains a varying amount of chemical matter and other constituents which have to undergo certain changes. Therefore, a wine containing more of each constituent will doubtless take longer to mature than a wine containing less. Certainly, with the minute amount of oxygen percolating through the pores of the wood, these changes take place more quickly than when the wine is stored in stone or glass jars when the oxygen can percolate only through the bung.

This is not to say that maturing is too quick when storing in barrels or that it is too slow when storing in jars. If slow maturing is best, then it would seem that jars, with only the bung to let oxygen through, would be ideal. But this is not so. Rather too little oxygen can get in through the bung.

The fact is that wood is best for maturing not only from the point of view of oxygen ingress but also for another reason. The wine absorbs beneficial substances from the wood, while the wood in turn absorbs a certain amount of harshness or perhaps tartness from the wine. Do not, however, think that wood will absorb too much of some constituent because it will not.

Even so, there comes a time when the wine should not be left in the wood any longer, simply because there is a risk of over-oxidation. This is the time when the wine has reached the point where sufficient oxidation has taken place and when the wine should be bottled to finish maturing. In the bottle important changes continue to take place. As I have mentioned these are not fully understood, which is the professsional way of saying that the process is still a complete mystery. When wines are bottled and sealed, further oxidation cannot take place, and the further chemical action, reaction and interaction, and the marrying of constituents can go on without risk of over-oxidation.

It is not possible for anybody to lay down hard and fast rules, or for that matter even hazard a guess as to when sufficient oxidation has taken place. Only the person who made the wine can judge, and he can only do this by tasting.

Tasting at this stage should show that the wine has mellowed and become much smoother and more wholesome. In fact, there should be a very noticeable change in the quality compared with that when the wine was first stored. And here it must rest with the individual as to when sufficient maturing in wood has taken place. Lighter wines usually mature more quickly than the heavier sorts. But neither develops much in the way of aroma or bouquet while in the wood, so do not expect this. As a rough guide, wines should be mellowed in wood for a year and then allowed to mature in bottle for a further year.

In bottle chemical action and reaction continue. Even though this is not fully understood, it is reasonable to suppose that chemical interaction is responsible for the changes which produce aromatic volatile esters which add remarkably to the aroma and bouquet of the wine. It is doubtful whether this would happen in the presence of oxygen, and it is therefore while stored in bottle that greater

(69)

changes take place. But whether the changes would take place successfully if wines were not allowed a mellowing period in the wood is another matter. It seems to me that, for the best results, the success of the improvement in bottle depends very much on the effectiveness of the period in the wood. But what of those who cannot use wooden containers for the early stage? Jars and ordinary bungs must be used and, as we have seen, the area of the bung allows for very little percolation of oxygen. This means that under these circumstances the first stage of maturing is likely to take a good deal longer than is desired. I think that this must be the reason for those jars of our grandparents' day that had bung-holes 7.5-10 cm (3-4 in) in diameter. These would certainly be more advantageous from the maturing point of view when jars must be used. Today most jars have bung-holes hardly more than 4 cm (1½ in) in diameter. So be it, we have to use them.

A certain amount of aeration could be effected by lifting the bung and replacing this with a firm knob of cotton wool for a few minutes every three months or so. If this is tried, the area around the bung and the bung itself must be well washed with sterilizing solution prior to removal. And, although jars of wine are usually stored in inaccessible places, it is best to do this without moving the jar, no matter how difficult this might be. I say this because I am convinced that one of the most important factors concerning successful maturing is non-disturbance.

Storing

Temperature and darkness are two very important factors here. There is very little the average amateur can do about storing in the ideal temperature simply because he has to store wherever he can. But it is worthwhile during the maturing period to attempt to keep the temperature fairly constant at around 10°C (50°F). This is impossible for most people who have to store in outhouses, cellars or under the stairs. But where central heating and a spare room are available, this should not prove too difficult.

Darkness is very important to most wines. Those stored in stone jars or in wood present no problem,.but those stored in glass jars which admit light must be kept in the dark. The effect of light is quite often disastrous. Direct light can quickly and irreparably ruin colour, flavour and bouquet, so that the wines simply are not worth a second tasting. Containers that admit light must therefore be kept in the dark. This is not to say that occasional opening of a door that admits light to the storage area would have a harmful effect; it would not. But prolonged exposure to moderate light certainly would.

Red wines are particularly susceptible to the effect of light: hence the need to store in the dark and in dark glass bottles. It does not matter if the bottles are dark brown or dark green, but clear or semi-clear glass should never be used.

The paler-coloured wines to the true whites seem unharmed by light, but I always take the precaution of never exposing them unnecessarily.

It is during storage that many beginners (and plenty of wine-makers with experience as well) come up against one big problem – that of re-fermentation. Yet this is a problem that should never arise. What usually happens is that the wine-maker discovers, much to his consternation, that a bung is missing from a jar. It may have popped out five minutes or a month earlier. Very often the wine is exposed to air for long periods without him knowing it. The result is that over-oxidation takes place or that the wine is attacked by wild yeasts or bacteria. Nearly always the wine is spoiled if exposure of this sort is prolonged.

It sometimes happens, when breaking the seal of a bottle, that the cork blows out and the wine fizzes up like champagne. Usually it is .cloudy and tastes awful. The simple explanation for this occurrence and for blown bungs is that fermentation was not complete when the wine was put in store.

Many, many wine-makers experience this and are dismayed, simply because they think the wine, which was quite good when put away, has gone wrong. Nothing has gone seriously wrong unless the wine has been spoilt owing to exposure to air or attack by yeast or bacteria. This depends on how long the bung has been missing. In the case of bottled products, refermenting in this fashion does no harm other than make the wine become cloudy.

When the bung blows from a jar, a fermentation lock must be fitted and the jar brought into the warm where it must remain until all renewed fermentation has ceased. When bottled products referment, the remainder of the batch must first be tracked down. Then the whole lot must be returned to a jar with a fermentation lock fitted and left in the warm.

The trouble in both cases is that fermentation stopped prematurely, most likely owing to cold in late autumn or early winter (see the section on sticking ferments, p. 31). This often happens when warmth is not given. The fermenting must becomes cold and cause the yeast to go dormant when, say, only 10% to 12% of alcohol has been made.

Later, when the warmth of spring penetrates to the wine, the yeast becomes active again. So all that is really happening is that fermentation is continuing from where it left off. This can be a confounded nuisance and a blessing in disguise at the same time. Always bear in mind that, provided spoilage yeasts or bacteria have not attacked the wine while the bung was missing, you will get a far better wine after this renewed fermentation.

Renewed fermentation is much easier to avoid, and can be prevented altogether, by using a fermentation cupboard as described on p. 33.

Preserving

It must be made clear at once that there should be no need to preserve well-made wines containing the maximum amount of alcohol. This is because there should be sufficient alcohol in the wine to preserve it.

However, it does sometimes happen that, in spite of good yeasts and a thoroughly good fermentation, the maximum alcohol is not made. It could be that you have missed the mark by as little as 1%. This may leave the wine less capable of combating disease, but it may also leave the yeast in a position to recommence fermentation, as we have just discussed.

Obviously before we go to the trouble of preserving wines it is as well to find out whether they are stable or not. If they are stable, then preserving is not necessary. But if, after the normal processes of fermentation, it is discovered that a wine is not stable, then preserving should be carried out. Either way, nothing in this line should be done until all fermentation has ceased in the normal way or until you are satisfied that the wine is a finished product ready to be put away to mature. Then, and only then, should the test be carried out to find whether the wine is stable or not. Users of the hydrometer should be able to verify whether they have made the maximum alcohol, so there should be no doubts for them. Even so, they may carry out the following simple test if only from the point of view of interest and practical experience.

Test for stability Almost every chemist will let you have cheaply two small test-tubes with a rubber or cork stopper for one of them. Or perhaps firms dealing in home wine-making equipment retail these now, although they used not to. Two small asprin or other very small bottles will do if nothing else is available. Thoroughly sterilize and rinse the tubes or bottles and shake them free of as much water as you can. Dry thoroughly otherwise one or two drops of water will dilute the sample and give an inaccurate reaction.

Half-fill both vessels with the wines to be tested. Cork and seal one tightly. Cut a small piece of flat, stiff card to a little larger than the top of the second container and rest this on top of it. Stand the samples side by side in a warm room for twenty-four hours. If both samples are exactly the same colour after this then the wine is stable and need not be preserved. On the other hand, if the unsealed sample has turned a darker colour, the wine is unstable and should be preserved.

Dry wines Thoroughly fermented-out, bone-dry wines, made with less sugar than produces the maximum alcohol, are another matter. All bone-dry wines are better for having a lower-than-average alcohol content, although many people make them to contain the maximum. But when they have been made to contain less than 14% of alcohol by volume, preserving should be carried out. This is not because they are likely to ferment again. They cannot do this simply because there is no unfermented sugar left. But there is always a risk of the acetic change taking place unless they are preserved.

This is not to say that the acetic change is automatic or even likely but it can happen. The risk comes during siphoning or racking in some other way, when these wines are exposed to the risk of contamination by the acetic bacteria. Bear in mind that the weaker the wine, the more susceptible it is to disease. On the whole, if bone-dry wines are handled carefully throughout and kept in containers which are full, there should be no risk whatsoever.

Chemical preservation   Chemical preservation is undoubtedly the cheapest and most reliable method. This is practised by the trade on a far wider scale than is generally imagined. Almost all wines are preserved. The low-alcohol wines are preserved chemically, while the higher-alcohol ones, such as sherries and ports, are fortified (or strengthened) with added alcohol. If this were not the case, there would be no high-alcohol wines simply because the trade cannot produce more alcohol in their wines by the normal processes of fermentation than we amateurs can, except perhaps by as little as 1% or 2%.

Sherries have spirit added at the end of fermentation, but port and a good many other wines have it added quite early in the process. When port, for example, is being fermented, skilled tasters sample by taste and by testing apparatus to ascertain the amount of sugar used up, the strength of flavour, the general sweetness to the palate and so on. When all these things are satisfactory, large amounts of spirit are added. This kills the yeast and therefore halts fermentation, and at the same time fortifies the wine to the percentage of alcohol required.

That is why the high-alcohol wines are so robust, so full of flavour and have such wonderful aroma and bouquet. Only the natural sugar in the grapes has been fermented, whereas we have to add sugar to produce the amount of alcohol we want. And for this we must use cane sugar. The trade have no need to do this for they utilize only a certain amount of the sugar the grapes contain. The rest is left unfermented. The added alcohol brings out the flavour and bouquet to the full. The added alcohol is what we pay for in the more expensive wines. The cheaper sorts, being preserved chemically, cost far less to produce.

Campden tablets are used for chemical preservation, and it is quite a simple matter to treat any amount of wine, however large or small, in this way. A well-made wine with a good percentage of alcohol, but one shown to be unstable by the test already mentioned, should not need more than one Campden tablet to every 5 l (1 gall). Crush this to powder in a small cup or glass with something not metal, such as the handle of a wooden spoon. Mix a little wine with it and stir the sample into the bulk. Cork the jar for twenty-four hours and repeat the test described earlier. You will know from this test whether or not a further tablet is necessary.

Two tablets are usually the maximum needed. Indeed, where delicately flavoured wines are preserved in this fashion, more than one tablet would be likely to affect the flavour. Wines with a full flavour would not be affected by a little more. When preserving in this fashion we are using the permitted preservative of sulphur dioxide. The amount allowed by law in wines in this country is 450 parts of preservative to 1,000,000 parts wine. This amount is represented by eight Campden tablets. From this we see that, in using two or even three tablets, we are well within the safety limits.

It is often with the sweet wines that more than two tablets are needed, especially if their alcohol content is low. This is because they are very liable to refermentation and very susceptible to disease. It is always best, therefore, to strive to make the maximum alcohol when making sweet wines, unless, of course, you like low-alcohol sweet wines. In this case, make them and then preserve.

Preserving with spirit   As mentioned, the higher-alcohol wines such as port are fortified during the process of fermentation not only to preserve them but also to retain their natural sugar content, to enhance their bouquet and to increase their alcohol content. This sort of thing is beyond the reach of the amateur because it is very expensive.

However we are able to increase the alcohol content by an important 2% or 3% at not too great expense when we have turned out exceptional wines worth preserving for themselves and keeping for many years. The addition of spirit will also bring about important improvements in aroma and bouquet during storage.

The trade use a number of brandies for this purpose, some of which are produced from the residue of a batch of perhaps thousands of gallons of wine – an enormous cake of skins and pips left after the wine has been drawn off. This cake is treated with water and allowed to ferment further. The resulting very poor wine, which has rather a low percentage of alcohol, is then distilled. Certain flavours and esters are allowed to come over during distillation so that this brandy has a flavour that makes it suitable for adding to a certain type of wine. But many brandies are produced which are quite neutral in both flavour and colour. This characteristic is often produced only by filtering the finished product through charcoal. When we talk of brandies, we immediately think of world-famous names, but almost all spirits distilled by the wine trade for fortification purposes are known as brandies.

It is with brandies quite neutral in both flavour and colour that we are likely to be interested. This is because when preserving wines we do not want to alter the colour or flavour of them. Rums, trade-named brandies such as the cognacs, whiskies and gins will all flavour wines and, in most cases, spoil them.

(74)

Imagine a well-made blackberry or elderberry wine with a hint of the flavour of rum, or even brandy for that matter. It would be quite out of character with the rest of the wine. It would be rather like taking good coffee and then detecting the taste of tea as you swallow it.

When fortifying or preserving, it is almost always best to use a spirit with neither colour or flavour. For this purpose, two grades of spirits are available: Polish pure spirit at 140° proof and vodka at 70° proof.

Before we go any further I think it is necessary to explain the difference between alcohol by volume and proof spirit, how these are compared with each other, and just what 'proof' means. This will clarify what is often one of the biggest mysteries confronting the average amateur.

When we refer to alcohol by volume, whether it be the amount in 250 l or 5 l, 50 gall or 1 gall, one bottle or half a glass, the percentage is the number of volumes of pure alcohol in each one hundred volumes of wine. Therefore, if we have half a glass of wine of 14% of alcohol by volume, we have fourteen volumes of pure alcohol in each hundred volumes. To put it another way, 100 l of the wine will contain 14 l of pure alcohol, and 100 gall will contain 14 gall.

The term 'proof' is a relic of ancient times when there was no accurate means of measuring the amount of alcohol present in liquors. Hence the confusion these days when accuracy is essential.

A liquor that is 100° proof spirit actually contains only 57% by volume, which is just over half of what the average person might imagine it to be. Gin of 70° proof has the more accurate corresponding figure of 40% by volume. A spirit of 175° proof is actually 100% by volume – pure alcohol. The following table may be useful. It does not cover the whole range as this is not necessary.

Relation between alcohol by volume and proof spirit

% Alcohol by volume	° Proof spirit
10	17.5
12	21
14	24.5
16	28
18	31.5
20	35
22	42.1
24	39
26	46
28	49.2
30	52.5
35	61.3
40	70

But it does cover the range which most amateurs may find useful for reference purposes from time to time.

When preserving with spirit, it is not necessary to add large amounts as all most of us want is to increase the alcohol content from the average of 14% by volume (24.5° proof) to about 16% by volume (28° proof). Indeed, this is all that is necessary for preservation purposes. You can, of course, increase the percentage further if you want to.

In the following tables, which show how much of various spirits to add to obtain a given percentage of alcohol, it is presumed that your wine contains 14% by volume. Any well-made wine should contain this amount or even 15%.

Here it is important to use the type of bottle relating to the table involved. British standard wine bottles and those containing gin and whisky (full-size bottles that is) hold about 7.5 dl (26 fl oz) when filled to the usual level. However bottles, especially those from Continental countries, hold 6 dl (1 pt or 20 fl oz) or a fraction more according to the type of bottle. Those tall bottles without shoulders are usually this size.

The tables are designed for fortifying one bottle at a time as this is the most that the average wine-maker will want to start with. The best means of adding the spirit is to' put it into an empty bottle and fill up with wine. To find the degrees proof corresponding to the percentage by volume given in these tables, see the table 'Relation between alcohol by volume and proof spirit' on p. 75.

Fortification Table 1
Using vodka to produce a bottle of fortified wine

Add x fl oz vodka	To x fl oz of wine of 14%	% alcohol by volume in the fortified wine
For a 6 dl (1 pt or 20 fl oz) bottle		
1	19	15.3
2	18	16.6
3	17	17.9
4	16	19.2
5	15	20.5
For a 7.5 dl (26 fl oz) standard British wine bottle		
1	25	15
2	24	16
3	23	17
4	22	18
5	21	19

Using vodka, as in the foregoing table, is convenient. Provided that the wines so treated have full flavour, the amounts of vodka added are unlikely to dilute the flavour to any noticeable extent. However this would not be true for wines with a delicate flavour. These include wines made from flowers or other ingredients that do not give such robust flavour as most English wild and garden fruits.

Where rather milder-flavoured wines are to be treated, and especially where more than 2 parts of vodka would be needed, some dilution of flavour is bound to result. It is therefore advisable to use a stronger spirit so that less is needed to do the job. The cost is the same whichever you use. Fortification Table 2 is for Polish pure spirit, which is obtainable from the suppliers listed at the end of the book.

Fortification Table 2
Using Polish pure spirit of 140% proof (80% by volume) to produce a bottle of fortified wine

Add x fl oz of spirit	To x fl oz of wine of 14%	% Alcohol by volume in the fortified wine
For a 6 dl (1 pt or 20 fl oz) bottle		
1	19	17.3
2	18	20.6
3	17	23.9
For a 7.5 dl (26 fl oz) standard British wine bottle		
1	25	16.5
2	24	19.1
3	23	21.6
4	22	24.2

Preserving Wine Ingredients
When I was a child (pity that's such a long time ago) my parents made thirty to forty gallons of wine at a time in what we called the outhouse, a built-on wooden affair stretching right along the back of the house with a window running the length of it. I can recall the vast tubs of fermenting wines and cider and the accompanying smells, wasps and flies – and of course the tales told later about such a such a batch being an absolute knock-out. Thirty, forty or fifty gallons at a time were common in my young days but they are not common today. Just a few bottles when the fruits are ripe or when the vegetables are ready. And it is sad to think that today so few people have that blessing, the scullery, outhouse, semi-basement or basement for that matter where vast amounts of wines could be started off (put down, we used to say) and kept out of the way until they were ready. It is sad too, to think that so much more wine could be made each season if people gathered more from hedgerow and garden and preserved them by one

of the many means available: turning them into jam (yes, and making wines with them later on if you want to), bottling them either by the heat treatment method or with a rather strong sulphite solution using Campden tablets (this incidentally is what Campden tablets were originally intended for, and I like to think that I was the first to use them in wine-making to destroy wild yeasts and bacteria on the fruits), drying them or deep-freezing them.

It may seem odd that many people make wines from jams that they have made themselves. They take into account how much sugar and fruit they used to make say 4.5 kg (10 lb) of jam and them make 10 l (2 gall) of wine with it, allowing for the sugar, of course, and then diluting with water accordingly.

So if you have an abundance of fruit or some spare vegetables that could be kept for wine-making at a later day, do consider preserving them in one way or another.

Fruits: most can be preserved in the wide-neck bottles known as preserving jars. They may be bottled in water or syrup. Certain fruits may be dried quite easily – apples, pears, bananas, apricots, blackberries, bilberries (whortleberries or herts), elderberries, blackcurrants, and many others.

Vegetables: beetroots, carrots, etc can be dried as well as beans such as broad and runner beans. Root vegetables being readily available at shops should not be preserved or stored unless you·grow them yourself and have a surplus.

Herbs: parsley, mint, borage, thyme and many other herbs and flowers including rose petals are quite easy to dry. Not all of these are used in wine-making, but it does show what can be done.

I often used to make wines with my preserved products, but this is not the place for a detailed description of the methods involved. Another book covering this should be consulted – there must be several in your local library. So if you have a surplus or can gather from the garden or hedgerow more than you can use at once, do think of preserving for wine-making at a later stage. I am sure you will be glad that you did.

7
MAKING WINES
IN A FLAT

With more and more people living in flats or other limited accommodation, there is an increasing need for recipes and methods that produce wines that can be ready in a short time, be used up quickly owing to shortage of storage space, and yet still be wines of reasonable quality. Let us copy the French and call them *vin ordinaire*.

In the ordinary way, with warmth during fermentation, these wines should be ready for bottling in about eight weeks from starting out and they should be quite drinkable a month or two later. So anybody starting off a 10 l (2 gall) batch at monthly intervals could easily have in a few short weeks a constant supply of sixteen bottles a month. If that is not enough, you will have to start off 15 l (3 gall) batches each month. If you want a much varied collection of wines it would be best to work with three or four 5 l (1 gall) batches of different sorts.

Naturally dry wines finish fermenting much sooner than the sweet sorts especially if only 900 g (2 lb) of sugar per 5 l (1 gall) are used. This will give you an alcohol content of 10.5% (17° proof). This is enough for dry wine. Such a wine might well ferment out in three weeks depending on the vigorousness of the yeast, the nutrient used and the temperature during fermentation. Indeed I have heard of wine-makers starting a batch of dry wine and winning first prize with it – believe it or not – six weeks later. All things are possible in wine-making. This wine would of course have been the lighter aperitif kind and to win a first prize it must have been of high standard in all respects. When making wines with the recipes in this chapter it would serve you well to use the hydrometer so that any sugar contained in the fruit (or, in the case of canned fruits in syrup, the amount of sugar in the syrup) can be accounted for before you add any; you may then calculate precisely how much to add to give you a total of 900 g (2 lb) per 5 l (1 gall) (see Chapter 5 'Using the Hydrometer', p. 56). A total of 900 g (2 lb) of sugar will give you an hydrometer reading of 1080.

If you do not like dry wines you will have to make them sweet. Or if you like rather lower-alcohol than average sweet wines you can make the dry wines and then sweeten them with ordinary sugar. But do bear in mind that this is almost certain to bring about renewed fermentation if the wines are kept for more than a week, especially if they are, for lack of cool storage space, kept in a warm temperature. A friend of mind in precisely this position who likes the lower-alcohol sweet wines (though not too sweet) makes all his wines dry, keeps them as dry wines because they will not ferment as such, and then sweetens three or four bottles at a time and keeps them in the fridge until he needs them. Personally, I don't like low-alcohol sweet wines. If I make sweet wines, which I sometimes do, I take good care to make all the alcohol that I can. But all this is a matter of taste. And therein lies, as I have written so many times before, the secret of successful wine-making: making what you like.

I can almost hear experienced wine-makers asking what is wrong with treating wines to prevent refermentation. Nothing, I suppose, but it is not something I would do if using the fridge suffices. But if you want to be sure of preventing refermentation without using the fridge, you can use one Campden tablet as suggested in the section on preserving on p. 71, or you may use one gramme of potassium sorbate, known commercially as Sorbistat K, per 5 l (1 gall). This amount should not be exceeded. You may be able to obtain this from your local wine supply shop. If not, Rogers Meads whose address is at the end of this book will supply you. Potassium sorbate has the effect of preventing the yeast from budding. Therefore any stray yeast spore that might be left in a dry wine would not be able to bud or reproduce and would therefore be unable to ferment the sweetening sugar.

Sweetening dry wines   There may be an easier method of sweetening finished dry wines, but I have not yet discovered it. When sweetening wines do be sure that they are brilliantly clear beforehand. How much sugar to add depends entirely on personal tastes. But it would be wise to use not more than two teaspoonsful of sugar per bottle, at least as a first treatment. Pour about one-third of the bottle of wine into a glass (Pyrex), china or polythene jug and add the sugar. Stand the jug in a saucepan of hot water over gentle heat and stir constantly to dissolve the sugar without letting the wine become too warm. When all the sugar is dissolved, pour the sample back into the bottle, using a funnel. If you propose to sweeten 5 l (1 gall), use one standard British Wine bottle of wine; add one or two teaspoonsful per bottle (six bottles per 5 l (1 gall)) and treat the sample as already described. Then pour the treated sample into a clean 5 l (1 gall) jar and add the rest of the wine to mix the sweetened sample thoroughly. Having treated either one bottle or the 5 l (1 gall), sample for sweetness. If more sugar is needed repeat the treatment, but use less sugar this time to ensure against over-sweetening.

If potassium sorbate (Sorbistat K) will prevent fermentation it would seem a better idea to make a wine that will turn out sweet and then sample daily after say two weeks' fermentation. As the yeast uses up the sugar the degree of sweetness can be defined either by taste (which, with the many flavours in a wine so young, might not be satisfactory) or by using the hydrometer to determine how much sugar is left unfermented. The Sorbistat K would then be added. However I am loth to use chemical additives at this stage of wine-making, even though this is an officially permissible additive. Using Campden tablets as a sterilizing agent at the beginning of winemaking is a different matter because the whole is lost during the process of wine-making, long before the wine is a finished product.

As most people living in flats live in towns or some distance from wild fruit, and as they of course have no garden fruits, I have confined the recipes in this chapter to the use of ingredients readily available at supermarkets or corner shops.

PINEAPPLE WINES

DRY
Fresh, fruity and very slightly acid.

two 450 g (15 oz) cans of pineapple rings or chunks; 225 g (½ lb) sultanas; 675 g (1½ lb) sugar; good wine yeast and nutrient; 3 dl (½ pt) freshly-made strong tea; few drops Pektolase; water as in method

SWEET
Nicely fruity with a slightly acid background.

two and a half 450 g (15 oz) cans (or the equivalent) pineapple rings or chunks; 225 g (½ lb) sultanas; 1.125 kg (2½ lb) sugar; good wine yeast and nutrient; 3 dl (½ pt) freshly-made strong tea; few drops Pektolase; water as in method

METHOD
Chop the pineapple pieces or mince them in a baby-food mincer and put them with the juice in the fermenting pail. Chop or mince the sultanas and mix them with the pulp. Put the sugar in about 1.2 l (2 pt) of water, bring to the boil stirring constantly to dissolve the sugar and then pour the boiling syrup over

(81)

the mixture. Make up to about 6 l (10 pt) with boiling water, cover closely and allow to cool to lukewarm.

The next step is to add the yeast, nutrient and tea. Cover the vessel with sheet polythene, tie this down tightly with thin strong string and put the mixture in the warm to ferment for ten days, stirring daily.

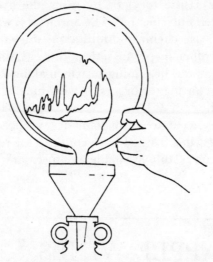

This illustration shows how to leave as much deposit behind as possible – a direction which appears in all my methods.

Having done this, strain the mixture through three or four thicknesses of muslin, pressing the pulp as dry as you can. Return the strained wine to the cleaned fermenting vessel and stir in the few drops of Pektolase. Cover as before and leave for a further three or four days in the warm.

Then pour carefully into a 5 l (1 gall) jar, leaving as much deposit in the pail as you can. If the jar is not filled to where the neck begins, fill to this level with boiled water. Then fit a fermentation lock and leave until all fermentation has ceased.

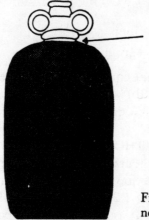

Fill the vessel to where the neck begins.

GRAPEFRUIT WINES

DRY

Very fresh aperitif with slightly acid background.

three 450 g (1 lb) cans of grapefruit segments (or the equivalent); 225 g (½ lb) sultanas; 675 g (1½ lb) sugar; 3 dl (½ pt) freshly-made strong tea; good wine yeast and nutrient; few drops Pektolase; water as in method

SWEET

450 g (1 lb) cans grapefruit segments (or the equivalent); 225 g (½ lb) sultanas; 1.225 kg (2¾ lb) sugar; 3 dl (½ pt) freshly-made strong tea; good wine yeast and nutrient; few drops Pektolase; water as in method

METHOD

Pour the contents of the cans into the fermenting pail, chop or mince the sultanas and mix them with the pulp. Then proceed in exactly the same way as given in the method for pineapple wine on p. 81.

BLACKBERRY WINES

Delicious deep-red wines with fresh fruity flavours

DRY

two 450 g (15 oz) cans of blackberries (or the equivalent); 225 g (½ lb) sultanas; 550 g (1¼ lb) sugar; strained juice of 1 lemon; few drops Pektolase; good wine yeast and nutrient; water as in method

SWEET

three 450 g (15 oz) cans blackberries (or the equivalent); 225 g (½ lb) sultanas; 1.125 kg (2½ lb) sugar; strained juice of 2 lemons; few drops Pektolase; good wine yeast and nutrient; water as in method

METHOD

Pour the contents of the cans into the fermenting vessel along with the chopped sultanas and strained lemon juice. Then proceed in exactly the same way as given in the method for pineapple wine on p. 81.

LOGANBERRY WINES
Delightfully fruity

DRY

two 450 g (15 oz) cans loganberries (or equivalent); 225 g (½ lb) sultanas; 775 g (1¾ lb) sugar; strained juice of 1 lemon; few drops Pektolase; good wine yeast and nutrient; water as in method

SWEET

three 450 g (15 oz) cans loganberries (or equivalent); 225 g (½ lb) sultanas; strained juice of 2 lemons; 1.125 kg (2½ lb) sugar; few drops Pektolase; good wine yeast and nutrient; water as in method

METHOD

Pour the contents of the cans into the fermenting pail along with the chopped sultanas and strained lemon juice. Then proceed in exactly the same way as given in the method for pineapple wine on p. 81.

LOGANBERRY AND BLACKBERRY WINES
A delicious blend of two very suitable fruits

DRY

one 450 g (15 oz) can of loganberries; one 450 g (15 oz) can blackberries; 225 g (½ lb) sultanas; 775 g (1¾ lb) sugar; strained juice of 1 lemon; few drops Pektolase; good wine yeast and nutrient; water as in method

SWEET

Make up about 600 g (22 oz) each of blackberries and loganberries (there is no need to be exact); 225 g (½ lb) sultanas; strained juice of 2 lemons; 2½ lb sugar; few drops Pektolase; good wine yeast and nutrient; water as in method

METHOD

Pour the contents of the cans into the fermenting pail along with the chopped sultanas and strained lemon juice. Then proceed in exactly the same way as given in the method for pineapple wine on p. 81.

PLUM WINES
Excellent wines with good flavour and colour

DRY
two 450 g (15 oz) cans of plums (or equivalent); 225 g (½ lb) sultanas; 775 g (1¾ lb) sugar; good wine yeast and nutrient; few drops Pektolase; water as in method

SWEET
three 450 g (15 oz) cans plums (or equivalent); 225 g (½ lb) sultanas; 1.125 kg (2½ lb) sugar; good wine yeast and nutrient; few drops Pektolase; water as in method

METHOD
Pour the contents of the cans into the fermenting pail along with the chopped sultanas. Then proceed in exactly the same way as given in the method for pineapple wine on p. 81.

PRUNE WINES
Wines of character and excellent colour

DRY
two 450 g (15 oz) cans prunes (or equivalent); 225 g (½ lb) dried currants; strained juice of 1 lemon; 775 g (1¾ lb) sugar; few drops Pektolase; good wine yeast and nutrient; water as in method

SWEET
three 450 g (15 oz) cans prunes (or equivalent); 225 g (½ lb) dried currants; strained juice of 2 lemons; 1.125 kg (2½ lb) sugar; few drops Pektolase; good wine yeast and nutrient; water as in method

METHOD
Pour the contents of the cans into the fermenting pail along with the chopped currants and strained lemon juice. Then proceed in exactly the same way as given in the method for pineapple wine on p. 81.

RASPBERRY WINES
Not one for making sweet, but as a really dry aperitif it is excellent

DRY
two 450 g (15 oz) cans of raspberries (or equivalent); 225 g (½ lb) sultanas; 675 g (1½ lb) sugar; few drops Pektolase; good wine yeast and nutrient; water as in method

METHOD
Pour the contents of the cans into the fermenting pail along with the chopped sultanas. Then proceed in exactly the same way as given in the method for pineapple wine on p. 81.

ORANGE WINES
An excellent dry wine quite unlike any commercial product and therefore unique. Do not make sweet

DRY
One can of Beech's prepared oranges (from wine supply shops); 225 g (½ lb) sultanas; 3 dl (½ pt) freshly-made strong tea; 675 g (1½ lb) sugar; few drops Pektolase; good wine yeast and nutrient; water as in method

METHOD
Pour the contents of the tin into the fermenting pail and add the ·chopped sultanas and tea. Then proceed in exactly the same way as given in the method for pineapple wine on p. 81.

See also the recipe for orange wine using fresh fruit on p. 119.

Making wines with concentrated grape juice Having made some, or perhaps all, the wines in this chapter most of you will think of varying the recipes and consider using concentrated grape juice instead of sultanas. Or perhaps you may want to use both. So the first thing to tell you is that the sugar in the sultanas has been accounted for. In other words the added sugar has been reduced to allow for the

100 g (¼ lb) sugar contained in 225 g (½ lb) sultanas. Therefore, if you decide to use 500 g (13 fl oz) of grape juice as well as the dried fruit, the amount of sugar given in the recipes would have to be reduced to allow for the sugar in the concentrate.

Example 1

Using 500 g (13 fl oz) grape juice as well as 225 g (½ lb) dried fruit. Reduce the amount of sugar by 350 g (13 oz) to allow for the sugar contained in the grape juice.

Example 2

Using 500 g (13 fl oz) without dried fruit. Reduce sugar given in recipe by 250 g (9 oz) to allow for the grape juice. Do bear in mind that 13 oz dry weight of sugar is not the same as the liquid measure, 13 fl oz of grape concentrate.

Type of concentrate to use with the recipes
> pineapple wines – hock
> grapefruit wines – hock
> blackberry wine (dry) – rosé
> blackberry wine (sweet) – Burgundy
> loganberry wines – rosé
> loganberry and blackberry wines – rosé or Burgundy
> plum wine (dry) – hock or rosé
> plum wine (sweet) – Burgundy or port style
> prune wines – grape juice not especially recommended
> raspberry wine – rosé
> orange wine – hock

Making wines with jam   Many people make quite good wines with jam – and even with marmalade though this is not something I have done myself. Anyway, it would be simple enough. Anybody with a stock of home-made jams would know how much fruit and how much sugar they used to produce the batch and work accordingly. Usually this is in the region of 450 g (1 lb) of sugar to 450 g (1 lb) of fruit. So a 450 g (1 lb) jar of jam would contain approximately 225 g (½ lb) of fruit and 225 g (½ lb) of sugar. And it would seem from this that 2.7 kg (6 lb) of jam would make 5 l (1 gall) of fairly full-flavoured wine from the fruit content point of view if nothing more by way of flavouring were added. However, this amount of jam would contain approximately 1.3 kg (3 lb) sugar and this, of course, is too much for a dry wine. So if you settle for say 1.8 kg (4 lb) of jam (roughly 900 kg (2 lb) of fruit) you would have approximately 900 g (2 lb) of sugar which is just right for a dry wine. But the 900 g (2 lb) of fruit is not enough for 5 l (1 gall) of well-flavoured wine. So if a little fresh fruit (or tinned fruit) of the same sort were added to make up the flavour it should come out quite well.

But with purchased jam the fruit and sugar content might not be the usual for the home-made varieties and it would therefore be necessary to use the hydrometer. In both cases the simple procedure would follow the same course. Firstly you would have to decide on the sort of jam – blackcurrant, blackberry or as your fancy takes you – and then decide how much you propose to use to make 5 l (1 gall), taking the fruit and sugar content into account, as I have just written. The jam would be put into the fermenting pail and the mixture brought up to 5 l (1 gall) with boiling water. Thorough stirring to break up the jam and disperse it throughout the water would be necessary. When this has been done it would be wise, when the mixture has cooled to about 15°C (60°F) to take the specific gravity to find the sugar content as already described in the chapter dealing with the hydrometer. But the sample for using the hydrometer would first have to be strained free of solids. Having taken the reading (specific gravity) you can consult the hydrometer table on p. 57 and decide whether to add more sugar or not. If you want to add some, bearing in mind that 65 g (2¼ oz) will raise the hydrometer reading by five, you may then go ahead. To dissolve the sugar, put about 6 dl (1 pt) of the diluted jam into a saucepan, put the sugar in this, heat gently, stirring frequently until the sugar is dissolved, and then stir this into the bulk.

The only addition would be one level 5 ml spoonful of citric acid stirred in together with a teaspoonful of Pektolase. This would be needed because jam contains a lot of pectin (if it did not, it would not set). Yeast and nutrient would then be added, the vessel covered as for other wines and fermentation allowed to proceed in the pail for ten days. After this the solids would have to be strained out, the strained wine returned to the cleaned fermenting pail and fermentation allowed to go on for a further three or four days, during which time most of the solids would settle out. The wine should then be poured carefully into a 5 l (1 gall) jar so that all the muddy deposit is left in the pail. A fermentation lock would then be fitted and the wine left to ferment to completion.

Making wines with jams and grape concentrate   Working on the principle that 1.3 kg (3 lb) of jam contain approximately 675 g (1½ lb) of fruit and 675 g (1½ lb) of sugar we are able to work out that the addition of 3.7 dl (13 fl oz) of a suitable grape concentrate will add a further 355 g (13 oz) of dry sugar (in suspension in the grape juice, of course). We are able to see that 1.3 kg (3 lb) of, say, blackberry jam and 3.7 dl (13 fl oz) of, say, Burgundy concentrate would give a decently flavoured wine. The mixture of grape juice and jam in this case would have a sugar content when mixed of approximately 1.025 kg (2 lb 5 oz), or perhaps a little less if the jam's sugar content is not as high as expected. The best way to work with such a combination would be to pour about 3.5 l (6 pt) of boiling water onto the jam in the fermenting pail, thoroughly mix it, allow it to cool (so as not to spoil the flavour of the grape juice to be added) and when cool add the grape juice. Having done that, make the mixture up to 5 l (1 gall) with boiled water that has cooled, take the reading (specific gravity) and proceed as already described. But less acid would be needed when concentrated grape juice is used because this contains a fair amount (about half of the amount needed in an ordinary wine), so one level 5 ml spoonful of citric acid would be enough. The same principle could be employed with any variety of jam that you might like to make into wine, but do remember to use Pektolase because all jams contain a lot of pectin.

Marmalade could be used in the same manner as jam, with, if you like, a concentrated grape juice, but in this case you would be limited to a hock type. Any red concentrate would be quite out of place with the flavour of marmalade oranges. Acid would not be needed because the marmalade and grape juice would give plenty into any wine. But when using marmalade some tannin would be needed, either in the form of 3 dl (½ pt) tea or a level teaspoonful of grape tannin dissolved before it is added to the must.

8

WINES FROM GARDEN AND HEDGEROW FRUITS:

Boiling Method

That Stewed Fruit Flavour

The boiling method lost most of its popularity when it was discovered that heating the fruits gave pectin into the wine to cause heavy and permanent cloudiness. This was, of course, before pectin-destroying enzymes came onto the market for general use by amateur wine-makers. It was owing to this that the sulphiting method came into its own. But because people like wines with the flavour of the fruits when stewed and because we now have Pectinol and Pektolase – two popular pectin-destroying enzymes which ensure a clear wine – the boiling method is fast becoming popular again.

I have found that most garden and hedgerow fruits are suitable for this method and I include recipes for each of them.

Preparing the fruits The methods call for prepared fruits. But first let me warn that it is wise not to gather fruits close to roads carrying heavy traffic because it has been proved that these contain lead from exhaust fumes. This is not to say that wines made from them would be dangerous, but the cumulative effect of drinking large quantities of wines made from them might prove harmful.

All that need be done by way of preparing the fruits is to remove stalks, hulls, leaves and so on and rinse them under a fast running tap.

All the recipes in this chapter are designed to make fully-flavoured, quite robust wines with a good bouquet and aroma without using any additional ingredients. However over the years since concentrated grape juices have become available many people, including myself, have been experimenting to find which concentrate goes best with which fruit and whether the addition made a worthwhile improvement to the wine. And most agree that there is an improvement (see also Chapter 16, 'Special additives'). It will be seen that under each recipe I recommend a certain amount of a certain type of concentrate. I add 'reduce sugar' by whatever amount is given. It is necessary to reduce the amount of sugar given in the recipes because the concentrate contains a lot and if we did not reduce it the wines would not turn out dry or medium as we want them and a sweet wine would be far too sweet.

Reminders Boiling the fruits and water as we do in this chapter destroys the wild yeast and bacteria on the fruits and any wild yeast there may be in the water so that we start off with a mixture free of the causes of spoilage. Do be careful to allow the boiled mixture to cool well before adding the yeast and pectin-destroying enzyme (Pektolase) otherwise both may be harmed and become ineffective.

It will be found that the sugar in the concentrated grape juice settles to the bottom of the can and becomes quite solid. It must be mixed with the juice before using. So open the can, stand it in hot water and stir until all the sugar is thoroughly mixed. Then measure the amount required.

All the recipes are for 5 l (1 gall) of wine. This is the amount most people like to use to get the feel of things before they embark on larger amounts. If you want to make two, three or four gallons merely increase the amount of each ingredient by the number of gallons you want to make.

Note that a 1 kg can of concentrated grape juice, the most-used size these days, contains 27 fl oz or 1 pt 7 fl oz. The 3.5 dl (13 fl oz) given under most recipes will be near enough half a 1 kg can. But bear in mind that the 35 oz *by weight* of 1 kg does not bear comparison with the *liquid* measure of 27 fl oz. So the 13 oz (350 g) of dry sugar is not the same as the 13 fl oz of grape juice.

BLACKCURRANT WINES
Burgundy style

DRY
1.3 kg (3 lb) blackcurrants; 1 kg (2¼ lb) sugar; good wine yeast and nutrient; level teaspoonful Pektolase; water as in method
3.5 dl (13 fl oz) Burgundy-style concentrate; reduce sugar by 350 g (13 oz)

MEDIUM
1.3 kg (3 lb) blackcurrants; 1.125 kg (2¾ lb) sugar; good wine yeast and nutrient; level teaspoonful Pektolase; water as in method
3.5 dl (13 fl oz) Burgundy-style concentrate; reduce sugar by 350 g (13 oz)

(91)

SWEET

1.3–1.6 kg (3–3½ lb) blackcurrants; 1.3 kg (3 lb) sugar; level teaspoonful Pektolase; good wine yeast and nutrient; water as in method
3.5 dl (13 fl oz) Burgundy-style concentrate; reduce sugar by 350 g (13 oz)

METHOD

Put the prepared fruits in a saucepan with enough water to cover them, bring slowly to the boil stirring frequently and then simmer till almost cooked. Put the sugar in the fermenting pail and pour over the hot fruit, stirring to dissolve the sugar. Then make up to about 5 l (1 gall) with boiling water. Stir well again. Allow the mixture to cool thoroughly and stir in the concentrated grape juice if being used. Add the yeast and nutrient. Give a thorough stirring, cover with sheet polythene with no holes in it, tie this down tightly with thin strong string and put the mixture in the warm to ferment for eight or nine days, stirring daily.

Having done this, strain the mixture through three or four thicknesses of muslin, wring out the pulp as dry as you can and discard it. Clean the fermenting pail and return the strained wine to this. Stir in the Pektolase. Cover as before and leave in the warm to ferment for a further three or four days.

The next step is to pour carefully into a 5 l (1 gall) jar leaving as much of the muddy deposit behind you as you can. If the jar is not filled to where the neck begins, fill to this level with boiled water, then fit a fermentation lock and leave until all fermentation has ceased.

LOGANBERRY WINES
Rosé types

DRY

1.3 kg (3 lb) loganberries; 900 g (2 lb) sugar; good wine yeast and nutrient; level teaspoonful Pektolase; water as in method
3.5 dl (13 fl oz) rosé concentrate; reduce sugar by 350 g (13 oz)

MEDIUM

1.3 kg (3 lb) loganberries; 1.125 kg (2½ lb) sugar; good wine yeast and nutrient; level teaspoonful Pektolase; water as in method
3.5 dl (13 fl oz) rosé concentrate; reduce sugar by 350 g (13 oz)

SWEET

1.8 kg (4 lb) loganberries; 1.225 kg (2¾ lb) sugar; level teaspoonful Pektolase; good wine yeast and nutrient; water as in method
3.5 dl (13 fl oz) rosé concentrate; reduce sugar by 350 g (13 oz)

METHOD
Proceed as for blackcurrant wine on p. 92.

BLACKBERRY WINES
Burgundy style, but different from Blackcurrant

DRY

1.6 kg (3½ lb) blackberries; 1 kg (2¼ lb) sugar; good wine yeast and nutrient; level teaspoonful Pektolase; water as in method
3.5 dl (13 fl oz) Burgundy-style concentrate; reduce sugar by 350 g (13 oz)

MEDIUM

1.8 kg (4 lb) blackberries; 1.125 kg (2½ lb) sugar; good wine yeast and nutrient; level teaspoonful Pektolase; water as in method
3.5 dl (13 fl oz) Burgundy-style concentrate; reduce sugar by 350 g (13 oz)

SWEET

2-2.5 kg (4½ -5 lb) blackberries; 1.225 kg (2¾ lb) sugar; level teaspoonful Pektolase; good wine yeast and nutrient; water as in method
3.5 dl (13 fl oz) Burgundy-style concentrate; reduce sugar by 350 g (13 oz)

METHOD
Proceed as for blackcurrant wine on p. 92.

GOOSEBERRY WINES
Excellent social hock types

DRY

1.3 kg (3 lb) gooseberries; 1 kg (2¼ lb) sugar; good wine yeast and nutrient; level teaspoonful Pektolase; water as in method
3.5 dl (13 fl oz) hock-style concentrate; reduce sugar by 350 g (13 oz)

MEDIUM

1.6 kg (3½ lb) gooseberries; 1.125 kg (2¼ lb) sugar; good wine yeast and nutrient; level teaspoonful Pektolase; water as in method
3.5 dl (13 fl oz) hock-style concentrate; reduce sugar by 350 g (13 oz)

SWEET

1.8-2 kg (4-4½ lb) gooseberries; 1.225 kg (2¾ lb) sugar; level teaspoonful Pektolase; good wine yeast and nutrient; water as in method
3.5 dl (13 fl oz) hock-style concentrate; reduce sugar by 350 g (13 oz)

METHOD

Proceed as for blackcurrant wine on p. 92.

DAMSON WINES

Outstanding wines of distinction

DRY

1.8-2.2 kg (4-5 lb) damsons; 1 kg (2¼ lb) sugar; good wine yeast and nutrient; level dessertspoonful Pektolase; water as in method
3.5 dl (13 fl oz) hock or rosé concentrate; reduce sugar by 350 g (13 oz)

MEDIUM

2.2-2.7 kg (5-6 lb) damsons; 1.125 kg (2¾ lb) sugar; good wine yeast and nutrient; level dessertspoonful Pektolase; water as in method
3.5 dl (13 fl oz) hock or rosé concentrate; reduce sugar by 350 g (13 oz)

SWEET

2.7-3.6 kg (6-8 lb) damsons; 1.350 kg (3 lb) sugar; good wine yeast and nutrient; level dessertspoonful Pektolase; water as in method
3.5 dl (13 fl oz) hock or rosé concentrate; reduce sugar by 350 g (13 oz)

METHOD

Proceed as for blackcurrant wine on p. 92.

ELDERBERRY WINES
Burgundy-port styles

DRY
900 g (2 lb) elderberries; 1.125 kg (2½ lb) sugar; good wine yeast and nutrient; level teaspoonful Pektolase; water as in method
3.5 dl (13 fl oz) Burgundy concentrate; reduce sugar by 350 g (13 oz)

MEDIUM
1.1 kg (2½ lb) elderberries; 1.225 kg (2¾ lb) sugar; good wine yeast and nutrient; level teaspoonful Pektolase; water as in method
3.5 dl (13 fl oz) Burgundy concentrate; reduce sugar by 350 g (13 oz)

SWEET
1.3-1.6 kg (3-3½ lb) elderberries; 1.350 kg (3 lb) sugar; good wine yeast and nutrient; level teaspoonful Pektolase; water as in method
3.5 dl (13 fl oz) port-style concentrate; reduce sugar by 350 g (13 oz)

METHOD
Proceed as for blackcurrant wine on p. 92, except that the first stage of fermentation should only last *five* days (instead of eight or nine) and the second stage should last *seven or eight* days (instead of three or four).

PLUM WINES
Rosé to Burgundy types

Victoria plums are excellent, but black plums or other sorts that are fully ripe may be used. Do not mix varieties.

DRY
2.2 kg (5 lb) plums; 1 kg (2¼ lb) sugar; good wine yeast and nutrient; level teaspoonful Pektolase; water as in method
3.5 dl (13 fl oz) rosé, hock or Burgundy concentrate; reduce sugar by 350 g (13 oz)

(95)

MEDIUM

2.7 kg (6 lb) plums; 1.125 kg (2½ lb) sugar; good wine yeast and nutrient; level teaspoonful Pektolase; water as in method
3.5 dl (13 fl oz) rosé, hock or Burgundy concentrate; reduce sugar by 350 g (13 oz)

SWEET

2.7-3.6 kg (6-8 lb) plums; 1.225 kg (2¾ lb) sugar; good wine yeast and nutrient; level teaspoonful Pektolase; water as in method
3.5 dl (13 fl oz) Burgundy or port-type concentrate; reduce sugar by 350 g (13 oz)

METHOD

Proceed as for blackcurrant wine on p. 92.

PEACH WINES

DRY

1.8 kg (4 lb) peaches; 1 kg (2¼ lb) sugar; good wine yeast and nutrient; level teaspoonful Pektolase; water as in method
3.5 dl (13 fl oz) hock-type concentrate; reduce sugar by 350 g (13 oz)

MEDIUM

2 kg (4½ lb) peaches; 1.125 kg (2½ lb) sugar; good wine yeast and nutrient; level teaspoonful Pektolase; water as in method
3.5 dl (13 fl oz) hock-type concentrate; reduce sugar by 350 g (13 oz)

SWEET

2.2 kg (5 lb) peaches; 1.225 kg (2¾ lb) sugar; good wine yeast and nutrient; level teaspoonful Pektolase; water as in method
3.5 dl (13 fl oz) rosé concentrate; reduce sugar by 350 g (13 oz)

METHOD

Halve the peaches, remove stones and peel all the peaches except two. The skins of the two impart a pleasant astringency.

Proceed as for blackcurrant wine on p. 92.

APRICOT WINES

DRY
1.8 kg (4 lb) apricots; 1 kg (2¼ lb) sugar; good wine yeast and nutrient; level teaspoonful Pektolase; water as in method
3.5 dl (13 fl oz) hock concentrate; reduce sugar by 350 g (13 oz)

MEDIUM
2 kg (4½ lb) apricots; 1.125 kg (2½ lb) sugar; good wine yeast and nutrient; level teaspoonful Pektolase; water as in method
3.5 dl (13 fl oz) hock-type concentrate; reduce sugar by 350 g (13 oz)

SWEET
2.2 kg (5 lb) apricots; 1.225 kg (2¾ lb) sugar; good wine yeast and nutrient; level teaspoonful Pektolase; water as in method
3.5 dl (13 fl oz) hock or rosé concentrate; reduce sugar by 350 g (13 oz)

METHOD
Halve the apricots and remove stones, but do not peel them.
Proceed as for blackcurrant wine on p. 92.

ELDERBERRY AND BLACKBERRY WINES
Burgundy-port styles

These blends of ingredients make for wine *par excellence*.

DRY
450 g (1 lb) elderberries; 1.125 kg (2½ lb) blackberries; 1.012 kg (2¼ lb) sugar; good wine yeast and nutrient; level teaspoonful Pektolase; water as in method
3.5 dl (13 fl oz) Burgundy concentrate; reduce sugar by 350 g (13 oz)

MEDIUM
450 g (1 lb) elderberries; 1.3 kg (3 lb) blackberries; 1.125 kg (2¾ lb) sugar; good wine yeast and nutrient; level teaspoonful Pektolase; water as in method
3.5 dl (13 fl oz) Burgundy concentrate; reduce sugar by 350 g (13 oz)

SWEET
675 g (1½ lb) elderberries; 1.6 kg (3½ lb) blackberries; 1.350 kg (3 lb) sugar; good wine yeast and nutrient; level teaspoonful Pektolase; water as in method
3.5 dl (13 fl oz) Burgundy or port-style concentrate; reduce sugar by 350 g (13 oz)

METHOD
Proceed as for blackcurrant wine on p. 92.

RASPBERRY WINES

DRY
1.125 kg (2½ lb) raspberries; 1.125 kg (2½ lb) sugar; good wine yeast and nutrient; level teaspoonful Pektolase; water as in method
3.5 dl (13 fl oz) rosé or hock concentrate; reduce sugar by 350 g (13 oz)

MEDIUM
1.3 kg (3 lb) raspberries; 1.225 kg (2¾ lb) sugar; good wine yeast and nutrient; level teaspoonful Pektolase; water as in method
3.5 dl (13 fl oz) rosé concentrate; reduce sugar by 350 g (13 oz)

SWEET
1.6 kg (3½ lb) raspberries; 1.350 kg (3 lb) sugar; good wine yeast and nutrient; level teaspoonful Pektolase; water as in method
3.5 dl (13 fl oz) hock-type concentrate; reduce sugar by 350 g (13 oz)

METHOD
Proceed as for blackcurrant wine on p. 92.

9
WINES FROM GARDEN AND HEDGEROW FRUITS:
Sulphiting Method

To Make Wines Easily Likened to Commercial Products

Wines made from garden and hedgerow fruits will always be the backbone of home wine-making. Despite the amount of building and road-making, there is still an abundance of wild fruits for the picking in most areas. But do take heed of the warning that fruits gathered from along main roads carrying heavy traffic are best avoided and try to gather them a few hundred metres away from such roads.

All the recipes in this chapter will make top-quality wines without any additional ingredients. However, as I have already said, over the years since concentrated grape juices have become available nearly everybody – including myself – has been experimenting with various types of of concentrated grape juice with various fruits, not only to find out whether there was any worthwhile improvement in the quality of the finished product, but also to find which concentrate goes best with which fruits. For example a Burgundy concentrate would not go well with loganberries, but makes for a better blackberry wine. This is easy to understand when you realize that blackberries used alone make for a Burgundy-type wine. (See also Chapter 16, 'Special Additives'.)

It will be seen that under each recipe I recommend a certain amount of a certain type of grape juice – rosé, hock or as the case may be. I also add 'reduce sugar by' whatever amount is given. The idea here is to show you which concentrate to use in what amount. Because the concentrate contains a lot of sugar, you will have to reduce the amount given in the recipes to allow for it. In this way you may use the recipes as they are if you want to. The use of concentrated grape juice with them is purely optional, because the recipes as they stand will make excellent wines in their own right. The methods call for prepared fruits. All you have to do is to remove leaves, stalks or hulls and rinse the fruits under a fast running tap. Do not bother to remove stones except from peaches and apricots.

(99)

The method in this chapter is what is known as the sulphiting method. Instead of heating the fruits or juices in order to destroy wild yeasts and bacteria on them we use Campden tablets. These, when crushed to a powder and dissolved in a small amount of water, make a small amount of liquid known as sulphite solution. This is the same as the sterilizing solution used for bottles and jars, but is much weaker. Do not be tempted to use a few drops of the sterilizing solution instead because you will not be able to control the amount of sulphite you add. By using Campden fruit-preserving tablets as in the methods we control the amount we use. This, it will be seen, is added when there is much less than 5 l (1 gall) of mixture. The idea here is to sterilize the fruits. Then when we make up the mixture to 5 l (1 gall) we dilute the sulphite in the mixture to a point where it will not prevent the yeast we add from making the mixture into wine for us. So we start off with a mixture free of all the causes of spoilage.

It will be seen that all the recipes are for 5 l (1 gall). This is the amount most people like to use to get the feel of things before making larger amounts. If you want to make larger amounts you will have to increase each ingredient according to the amount you want. If you want 10 l (2 gall), double all ingredients. If you want 25 l (5 gall) increase all ingredients to five times the amounts given.

Reminders For many years now I have recommended using boiled water that has cooled. 5 l (1 gall) of boiled water takes a long time to cool, so it would be wise to boil this several hours before starting to make the wine. Similarly, sugar boiled in water to make syrup needs a couple of hours to cool, so you can make this up ready for use when required in the methods. Many people seem to get along fine without boiling their water, but I prefer to do this (my water supply is not suspect, incidentally), and certainly I get a better wine than when I use it straight from the tap.

If you use concentrated grape juice with the recipes in this chapter the can must be opened, stood in hot water and stirred to dissolve the grape sugar which settles to the bottom. The amount to use may then be poured into the mixture when advised in the method.

Note that the popular 1 kg can of concentrated grape juice contains about 7 dl (27 fl oz), so the 3.5 dl 13 fl oz given under each recipe is near enough half a 1 kg can. Do not confuse the 35 oz *by weight* of 1 kg with the *liquid* measure of 27 fl oz; the 13 oz of dry sugar is not the same as the 13 fl oz of grape juice.

BLACKBERRY WINES

DRY
Good imitation of Beaujolais.
1.3 kg (3 lb) blackberries; 225 g (½ lb) elderberries; 1 kg (2¼ lb) sugar; good wine yeast and nutrient; water as in method
3.5 dl (13 fl oz) of Burgundy concentrate; reduce sugar by 350 g (13 oz)

MEDIUM
Burgundy style.
2 kg (4½ lb) blackberries; 1.225 kg (2¾ lb) sugar; good wine yeast and nutrient; water as in method

SWEET
Sweeter Burgundy style.
2.2 kg (5 lb) blackberries; 1.350 kg (3 lb) sugar; good wine yeast and nutrient; water as in method
3.5 dl (13 fl oz) Burgundy concentrate; reduce sugar by 350 g (13 oz)

SPECIAL
Excellent port style. Include the concentrate, but do not reduce sugar.
1.6 kg (3½ lb) blackberries; 450 g (1 lb) elderberries; 3.5 dl (13 fl oz) port-style concentrate; good wine yeast and nutrient; 1.125 kg (2½ lb) sugar; water as in method

METHOD
Put the prepared fruits in the fermenting pail and crush well by hand and stir in about 2½ l (½ gall) of boiled water that has cooled. Crush one Campden fruit-preserving tablet to a powder, dissolve this in about an eggcupful of warm water and stir it into the mixture. Add the concentrated grape juice, if being used, and give a thorough stirring. Put the sugar in about 1.2 l (2 pt) of water, bring to the boil slowly stirring constantly until dissolved, allow to cool and then stir into the rest. Having done this, add the yeast and nutrient.

The next step is to cover with sheet polythene with no holes in it, tie this down tightly with thin strong string and ferment in the warm for eight or nine days, stirring daily. After this, strain the mixture through three or four thicknesses of muslin, press the pulp as dry as you can and discard it. Clean the fermenting pail and return the strained wine to this. Cover as before and leave in the warm to continue fermenting for three or four more days. The next step is to pour carefully into a 5 l (1 gall) jar leaving as much of the muddy deposit in the pail as you can. If the jar is not filled to where the neck begins, fill to this level with boiled water, then fit a fermentation lock and leave until all fermentation has ceased.

ELDERBERRY WINES

Use elderberries growing in small round clusters, not those in large irregular-shaped clusters.

DRY
900 g (2 lb) elderberries; 1 kg (2¼ lb) sugar; good wine yeast and nutrient; water as in method
3.5 dl (13 fl oz) Burgundy concentrate; reduce sugar by 350 g (13 oz)

MEDIUM
Often likened to Dubonnet. 1.3 kg (3 lb) elderberries; 1.225 kg (2¾ lb) sugar; good wine yeast and nutrient; water as in method
Either 3.5 dl (13 fl oz) Burgundy concentrate; reduce sugar by 350 g (13 oz) *or* 1.4 dl (5 fl oz) Tamilier concentrate; if you use the latter do not reduce the sugar.

SWEET
Port style. 1.8 kg (4 lb) elderberries; 1.350 kg (3 lb) sugar; good wine yeast and nutrient; water as in method
3.5 dl (13 fl oz) port-type concentrate; reduce sugar by 350 g (13 oz)

SPECIAL
Do not omit the concentrate. Do not reduce amounts of sugar stated. 450 g (1 lb) elderberries; 900 g (2 lb) blackberries; 2.8 dl (10 fl oz) Tamalier concentrate; good wine yeast and nutrient; water as in method; sugar: for dry use 1 kg (2¼ lb); for medium use 1.225 kg (2¾ lb); for sweet use 1.350 kg (3 lb)

METHOD
Proceed as for blackberry wine on p. 101.

(102)

DAMSON WINES

DRY
Table wine.
1.8 kg (4 lb) damsons; 1 kg (2¼ lb) sugar; good wine yeast and nutrient; water as in method
3.5 dl (13 fl oz) rose concentrate; reduce sugar by 350 g (13 oz)

MEDIUM
2.2 kg (5 lb) damsons; 1.225 kg (2¾ lb) sugar; good wine yeast and nutrient; water as in method
3.5 dl (13 fl oz) rosé concentrate; reduce sugar by 350 g (13 oz)

SWEET
2.7-3.8 kg (6-8 lb) damsons; 1.350 kg (3 lb) sugar; good wine yeast and nutrient; water as in method
Use two Campden tablets owing to larger amount of fruits.
3.5 dl (13 fl oz) Burgundy concentrate; reduce sugar by 350 g (13 oz)

SPECIAL
Do not omit the concentrate and do not reduce the sugar.
2.2 kg (5 lb) damsons; 2.8 dl (10 fl oz) Tamalier concentrate; good wine yeast and nutrient; water as in method; sugar: for dry use 1 kg (2¼ lb); for medium use 1.225 kg (2¾ lb); for sweet use 1.350 kg (3 lb)

METHOD
Proceed as for blackberry wine on p. 101.

PLUM WINES

Any variety of fully ripe plums may be used, but do not mix varieties. Black or near black sorts are best.

DRY

Table wine. 1.8 kg (4 lb) plums; 900 g (2 lb) sugar; good wine yeast and nutrient; water as in method
3.5 dl (13 fl oz) Burgundy concentrate; reduce sugar by 350 g (13 oz)

MEDIUM

2.2-2.7 kg (5-6 lb) plums; 1.225 kg (2¾ lb) sugar; good wine yeast and nutrient; water as in method
3.5 dl (13 fl oz) Burgundy concentrate; reduce sugar by 350 g (13 oz)

SWEET

Full-bodied heavier sort. 3.6 kg (8 lb) plums; 1.350 kg (3 lb) sugar; good wine yeast and nutrient; water as in method.
Use two Campden tablets owing to larger amount of fruit.
3.5 dl (13 fl oz) Burgundy concentrate; reduce sugar by 350 g (13 oz)

SPECIAL

Excellent port style. Do not omit the concentrate and do not reduce the sugar.
2.7 kg (6 lb) plums; 450 g (1 lb) elderberries; 3.5 dl (13 fl oz) port-style concentrate; 1.125 kg (2½ lb) sugar; good wine yeast and nutrient; water as in method

METHOD

Proceed as for blackberry wine on p. 101.

GREEN GOOSEBERRY WINES

Slightly acid wines, excellent as an aperitif when made dry.

DRY

1.3 kg (3 lb) gooseberries; 1.125 kg (2½ lb) sugar; good wine yeast and nutrient; water as in method
3.5 dl (13 fl oz) hock or rosé concentrate; reduce sugar by 350 g (13 oz)

MEDIUM

1.6 kg (3½ lb) gooseberries; 1.225 kg (2¾ lb) sugar; good wine yeast and nutrient; water as in method
3.5 dl (13 fl oz) hock or rosé concentrate; reduce sugar by 350 g (13 oz)

SWEET

1.8 kg (4 lb) gooseberries; 1.350 kg (3 lb) sugar; good wine yeast and nutrient; water as in method
3.5 dl (13 fl oz) hock concentrate; reduce sugar by 350 g (13 oz)

METHOD

Proceed as for blackberry wine on p. 101.

BLACKCURRANT WINES

DRY

1.1 kg (2½ lb) blackcurrants; 1 kg (2¼ lb) sugar; good wine yeast and nutrient; water as in method
1.4 dl (5 fl oz) of Tamalier concentrate; do not reduce sugar.

MEDIUM

1.3 kg (3 lb) blackcurrants; 1.225 kg (2¾ lb) sugar; good wine yeast and nutrient; water as in method
1.4 dl (5 fl oz) Tamalier concentrate; do not reduce sugar

SWEET

1.8 kg (4 lb) blackcurrants; 1.350 kg (3 lb) sugar; good wine yeast and nutrient; water as in method
2.8 dl (10 fl oz) Tamalier concentrate; do not reduce sugar.

METHOD

Proceed as for blackberry wine on p. 101.

REDCURRANT WINES

DRY

1.1 kg (2½ lb) redcurrants; 1 kg (2¼ lb) sugar; good wine yeast and nutrient; water as in method
3.5 dl (13 fl oz) rosé concentrate; reduce sugar by 350 g (13 oz)

MEDIUM

1.3 kg (3 lb) redcurrants; 1.225 kg (2¾ lb) sugar; good wine yeast and nutrient; water as in method
3.5 dl (13 fl oz) rosé concentrate; reduce sugar by 350 g (13 oz)

SWEET

1.6 kg (3½ lb) redcurrants; 1.350 kg (3 lb) sugar; good wine yeast and nutrient; water as in method
3.5 dl (13 fl oz) rosé concentrate; reduce sugar by 350 g (13 oz)

METHOD

Proceed as for blackberry wine on p. 101.

APRICOT WINES

Halve the apricots and remove stones before weighing fruit.

DRY

1.1 kg (2½ lb) stoned apricots; 1 kg (2¼ lb) sugar; good wine yeast and nutrient; water as in method
3.5 dl (13 fl oz) rosé or hock concentrate; reduce sugar by 350 g (13 oz)

MEDIUM

1.3 kg (3 lb) stoned apricots; 1.225 kg (2¾ lb) sugar; good wine yeast and nutrient; water as in method
3.5 dl (13 fl oz) hock concentrate; reduce sugar by 350 g (13 oz)

SWEET

1.6 kg (3½ lb) stoned apricots; 1.350 kg (3 lb) sugar; good wine yeast and nutrient; water as in method
3.5 dl (13 fl oz) hock concentrate; reduce sugar by 350 g (13 oz)

METHOD

Proceed as for blackberry wine on p. 101.

LOGANBERRY WINES

DRY
1.1 kg (2½ lb) loganberries; 1 kg (2¼ lb) sugar; good wine yeast and nutrient; water as in method
3.5 dl (13 fl oz) rose concentrate; reduce sugar by 350 g (13 oz)

MEDIUM
1.3 kg (3 lb) loganberries; 1.225 kg (2¾ lb) sugar; good wine yeast and nutrient; water as in method
3.5 dl (13 fl oz) rosé concentrate; reduce sugar by 350 g (13 oz)

SWEET
1.3 kg (3 lb) loganberries; 1.3 kg (3 lb) sugar; good wine yeast and nutrient; water as in method
3.5 dl (13 fl oz) hock concentrate; reduce sugar by 350 g (13 oz)

METHOD
Proceed as for blackberry wine on p. 101.

10
MAKING WINES
WITH VEGETABLES

I did for a long time believe that with so many modern ingredients available today for making top-class wines so easily and quickly the somewhat tedious chore of preparing vegetables for wine-making would be too much for anybody. But I was wrong. Visits to wine-making clubs where vegetable wines are still proffered proved this. I find that in most parts of the country indeed, even where the hurtling speed of big town life leaves so little time to spare, plenty of people are quite happy to scrub and grate their parsnips, potatoes and carrots to make incomparable wines.

I think the reason that these wines are popular is that similar wines cannot be bought. It is all very well to make wines like those that can be bought at any off-licence, but it is not very difficult considering the ingredients available for making imitations of commercial products. However to make wines that are true country wines, the like of which cannot be found anywhere else, is something quite out of the ordinary. Indeed, wines made from the recipes in this chapter, as well as wines made from flowers (Chapter 12), are unique. And what is more, each hobbyist develops a technique or knack of making some really exceptional wines that concentrated grape juice addicts would scoff at – but only because of a bit of snobbery that has grown up around the latest generation of wine-makers who have not tasted a true country wine of real quality and perhaps never will. They smugly think that because they use imported concentrated grape juices their wines are real wines while those made with anything else are not. I have met them. I pity them. I am certain that if they made a really good carrot, or parsnip or other vegetable wine and were able to wait for it to develop – and I will confess that this often takes a long time – they might take another look at the cost of concentrated grape juice.

Vegetable wines, as I have suggested above, need at least a year to develop their full flavour, aroma and most of their quality. Given two years to come along, they really are very excellent wines, full of flavour, with a bouquet quite unique and a fullness and robustness that surprises many. And if you don't watch the amount you drink at one sitting, they'll put you flat on your back when you still think you are only half way along the road.

Vegetable wines made from roots such as potatoes or parsnips often present the maker with a clearing problem. This is caused by starch in the roots being boiled into the water, with the boiling that is necessary to destroy soil bacteria. One means of overcoming this problem is to starve the yeast of sugar during the earliest stages of fermentation. This will induce the yeast to convert the starch to sugar and ferment it out leaving a clear wine. This is why I recommend adding the sugar in two stages in certain of the following methods.

Unfortunately this little scheme does not always work. It is then that we have to resort to the use of a starch-destroying enzyme, known as fungal amylase. Starch, like pectin (in fruits) holds minute solids in suspension to form the cloudiness. Destroy the starch and the solids forming the cloud settle out. But it is worth waiting to see if the starve-the-yeast plan has worked before doing this. If your vegetable wines are still cloudy say a week after fermentation has ceased use of starch-destroying enzyme would be justified. The amount suggested by the manufacturers is 2.5 g per 25 l (5 gall). This amount is represented by one capful, using the cap on the bottle it is supplied in. If you are treating 5 l (1 gall) put a capful on a piece of clean paper and divide into four. Then mix a quarter with the wine. This is a trifle more than is needed, but it will do no harm. If you mix the amount to be used with a little wine and then stir it into the bulk, the wine should be clear in a day or so.

It will be seen that I recommend the use of dried fruits with the recipes in this chapter. This is because without them the wines would lack character and fullness, and, what is more, fermentation would not be so good. Acid in the form of citric acid obtainable from a chemist very cheaply is also needed because roots contain none. Tannin in the form of strong tea is needed for the same reason, but you can add a pinch of grape tannin instead of tea if you want to.

If you want to use concentrated grape juice in the recipes instead of dried fruit you may do so. For this reason I have added under each recipe the name of a concentrate and how to alter the sugar amounts given in the recipes to allow for the sugar contained in the grape juice, bearing in mind that the dried fruits contain roughly 225 g (½ lb) sugar per 450 g (1 lb) fruit. For example, if you leave out 450 g (1 lb) of raisins, you will have to add a 225 g (½ lb) sugar to make up for them because the sugar content of the fruits has been allowed for in the recipes. But if you add 3.5 dl (13 fl oz) grape concentrate, as recommended in other chapters, you will have to reduce the sugar by 350 g (13 oz dry weight). So if you use grape juice instead of dried fruit, you would in fact have to reduce the sugar stated in the recipe by 125 g (5 oz). You will find clear instructions under each recipe as you come to it.

Do bear in mind that the *dry* measure of 13 oz of sugar is not the same as the *liquid* measure of 13 fl oz of concentrate.

POTATO WINES

King Edward potatoes are best. Do not make dry potato wine.

MEDIUM
900 g (2 lb) old potatoes; 450 g (1 lb) raisins; 3 oranges; 1 level 5 ml spoonful citric acid; 3 dl (½ pt) freshly made strong tea; 1 kg (2¼ lb) sugar; good wine yeast and nutrient; water as in method
If using grape juice instead of raisins, use 3.5 dl (13 fl oz) hock type and reduce sugar by 125 g (5 oz)

SWEET
900 g (2 lb) old potatoes; 450 g (1 lb) raisins; 3 oranges; 1 level 5 ml spoonful citric acid; 3 dl (½ pt) freshly made strong tea; 1.250 kg (2¾ lb) sugar; good wine yeast and nutrient; water as in method below
If using grape juice instead of raisins, use 3.5 dl (13 fl oz) hock type and reduce sugar by 125 g (5 oz)

METHOD
Do not peel potatoes but scrub them thoroughly removing eyes and crevices. Cut them up finely or grate them. Put them in about 2½ l (4 pt) of water, bring slowly to the boil and simmer gently for fifteen minutes by the clock, taking off all scum that rises. Put roughly half the sugar in the fermenting pail with the chopped raisins. (If using grape juice instead of raisins it is added later.) Strain the boiling potatoes onto them through three or four thicknesses of butter muslin. Allow to drain for a few minutes and then press well. Stir thoroughly to dissolve the sugar, cover closely and leave the mixture to cool to lukewarm or about 18°C (65°F).

The next step is to add the acid and tea. Then halve the oranges, press out the juice, strain it free of pips and stir it into the mixture. If grape juice is being used, this is the time to stir it in. Having done this, make the mixture up to roughly 5 l (1 gall) with boiled cooled water, then add the yeast and nutrient. Cover the vessel with sheet polythene, tie it down tightly with thin strong string (or fit the lid) and put the vessel in a warm place to ferment for eight or nine days, stirring daily.

Now strain out the solids through three or four thicknesses of muslin. Wring them out as dry as you can and return the wine to the cleaned fermenting pail.

Straining hot ingredients
To prevent accidents tie one cloth to the pail – allowing sufficient sag – and lay a second cloth on top. The hot solids may then be lifted off safely.

Put the remaining sugar in about 6 dl (1 pt) of hot water in a saucepan and bring it slowly to the boil, stirring constantly to prevent burning. Allow this to cool and then stir it into the wine. Cover as before, leave in the warm for a further three or four days and then pour gently into a 5 l (1 gall) jar, leaving as much deposit in the pail as you can. If the jar is not filled to where the neck begins, fill to this level with boiled water, then fit a fermentation lock and leave in the warm until all fermentation has ceased.

Note on the above method
If you use grape juice instead of raisins, there will be no solids to strain out. So after eight or nine days, merely add the remaining sugar as advised above and proceed from there.

PARSNIP WINES

Do not make dry parsnip wine. Use parsnips that are old crop rather than new.

MEDIUM
1.3 kg (3 lb) parsnips; 450 g (1 lb) sultanas; 1 kg (2¼ lb) sugar; 2 oranges; 1 level 5 ml spoonful citric acid; 3 dl (½ pt) freshly made strong tea; good wine yeast and nutrient; water as in method
If using grape juice instead of sultanas, use 3.5 dl (13 fl oz) hock type and reduce the sugar by 125 g (5 oz)

SWEET
1.8 kg (4 lb) parsnips; 450 g (1 lb) sultanas; 1.125 kg (2½ lb) sugar; 2 oranges; 1 level 5 ml spoonful citric acid; 3 dl (½ pt) freshly made strong tea; good wine yeast and nutrient; water as in method
If using grape juice instead of sultanas, use 3.5 dl (13 fl oz) hock type and reduce the sugar by 125 g (5 oz)

METHOD
Proceed as for potato wine on p. 110.

CARROT WINES

A great favourite with an enormous number of people.

DRY
1.8 kg (4 lb) carrots; 450 g (1 lb) sultanas; 2 oranges; 1 level 5 ml spoonful citric acid; 775 g (1¾ lb) sugar; 3 dl (½ pt) freshly made strong tea; good wine yeast and nutrient; water as in method
If using grape juice instead of sultanas, use 3.5 dl (13 fl oz) rose and reduce the sugar by 125 g (5 oz)

MEDIUM
1.8 kg (4 lb) carrots; 450 g (1 lb) sultanas; 2 oranges; 1 level 5 ml spoonful citric acid; 1 kg (2¼ lb) sugar; 3 dl (½ pt) freshly made strong tea; good wine yeast and nutrient; water as in method
If using grape juice instead of sultanas, use 3.5 dl (13 fl oz) rosé and reduce the sugar by 125 g (5 oz)

SWEET
2.2 kg (5 lb) carrots; 450 g (1 lb) sultanas; 3 oranges; 1 level 5 ml spoonful

citric acid; 1.125 kg (2½ lb) sugar; 3 dl (½ pt) freshly made strong tea; good wine yeast and nutrient; water as in method

If using concentrated grape juice instead of sultanas, use 3.5 dl (13 fl oz) rosé and reduce the sugar by 125 g (5 oz)

METHOD

Proceed as for potato wine on p. 110.

MANGOLD (OR MANGEL-WURZEL) WINES

A real old country favourite, having been made for centuries and still very popular today. Mangolds are obtainable from farms.

Follow exactly the recipes for carrot wine using mangolds instead of carrots, and follow the method for potato wine on p. 110.

BEETROOT WINES

Yet another real country wine and still a favourite. Using young beets and be sure to keep the wine in the dark or in dark glass bottles otherwise it will lose its colour and character.

DRY

1.3 kg (3 lb) beetroots; 450 g (1 lb) raisins; 2 oranges; 1 level 5 ml spoonful citric acid; 775 g (1¾ lb) sugar; 3 dl (½ pt) freshly made strong tea; good wine yeast and nutrient; water as in method.

If using grape juice instead of raisins, use 3.5 dl (13 fl oz) Burgundy type and reduce sugar by 125 g (5 oz)

MEDIUM

1.6 kg (3½ lb) beetroots; 450 g (1 lb) raisins; 2 oranges; 1 level 5 ml spoonful citric acid; 1 kg (2¼ lb) sugar; 3 dl (½ pt) freshly made strong tea; good wine

yeast and nutrient; water as in method
If using grape juice instead of raisins, use 3.5 dl (13 fl oz) Burgundy type and reduce sugar by 125 g (5 oz)

SWEET

1.8 kg (4 lb) beetroots; 450 g (1 lb) raisins; 3 oranges; 1 level 5 ml spoonful citric acid; 1.125 kg (2½ lb) sugar; 3 dl (½ pt) freshly made strong tea; good wine yeast and nutrient; water as in method
If using grape juice instead of raisins, use 3.5 dl (13 fl oz) Burgundy type and reduce sugar by 125 g (5 oz)

METHOD

Proceed as for potato wine on p. 110.

PEA-POD WINES

Another true country wine still very popular today. Do not allow one pea, however small, into the mixture.

DRY

900 g (2 lb) pea-pods; 450 g (1 lb) sultanas; 2 oranges; 1 level 5 ml spoonful citric acid; 775 g (1¾ lb) sugar; 3 dl (½ pt) freshly made strong tea; few drops Pektolase; good wine yeast and nutrient; water as in method
If using grape juice instead of sultanas, use 3.5 dl (13 fl oz) hock type and reduce sugar by 125 g (5 oz)

MEDIUM

900 g (2 lb) pea-pods; 450 g (1 lb) sultanas; 2 oranges; 1 level 5 ml spoonful citric acid; 1 kg (2¼ lb) sugar; 3 dl (½ pt) freshly made strong tea; few drops Pektolase; good wine yeast and nutrient; water as in method
If using grape juice instead of sultanas, use 3.5 dl (13 fl oz) hock type and reduce sugar by 125 g (5 oz)

SWEET

1.1 kg (2½ lb) pea-pods; 450 g (1 lb) sultanas; 1.125 kg (2½ lb) sugar; 3 oranges; 1 level 5 ml spoonful citric acid; 3 dl (½ pt) freshly made strong tea; few drops Pektolase; good wine yeast and nutrient; water as in method

If using grape juice instead of sultanas, use 3.5 dl (13 fl oz) hock type and reduce sugar by 125 g (5 oz)

METHOD

Thoroughly wash the pea-pods and cut them up quite small. Put them in enough water to cover them well, bring slowly to the boil and simmer gently for twenty minutes with the lid on. Put the sugar in the fermenting pail with the chopped sultanas (but do not add grape juice at this stage, if being used). Strain the boiling pea-pods over the sugar and sultanas through three or four thicknesses of muslin. Allow to drain, squeeze out the maximum liquor and discard the pods. Stir the mixture to dissolve the sugar, and make up to about 5 l (1 gall) with boiling water. Add the citric acid and tea, cover closely and allow the mixture to cool to about 18°c (65°F) – lukewarm. Halve the oranges, squeeze out the juice, strain and stir into the mixture. Then add the yeast, nutrient and the few drops of Pektolase. Then stir in the grape juice if being used. Cover the vessel with sheet polythene (or fit the lid) and tie this down tightly with thin strong string. Having done this put the vessel in the warm to ferment for ten days, stirring daily. The next step is to strain out the solids through several thicknesses of muslin, clean the fermenting vessel and return the strained wine to this. Cover as before and leave in the warm to ferment for a further three or four days.

Then pour carefully into a 5 l (1 gall) jar leaving as much deposit in the pail as you can. Fill the jar to where the neck begins with boiled water that has cooled, then fit a fermentation lock and leave until all fermentation has ceased.

RUNNER BEAN WINES

These are surprisingly good wines which are still very popular in country areas or wherever they are grown.

DRY

900 g (2 lb) runner beans; 450 g (1 lb) sultanas; 775 g (1¾ lb) sugar; two medium-sized grapefruit (or equivalent of tinned grapefruit); 3 dl (½ pt) freshly made strong tea; few drops Pektolase; good wine yeast and nutrient; water as in method

If using grape juice instead of sultanas, use 3.5 dl (13 fl oz) hock type and reduce sugar by 125 g (5 oz)

MEDIUM

900 g (2 lb) runner beans; 450 g (1 lb) sultanas; 2 medium-sized grapefruit (or equivalent of tinned grapefruit); 1 kg (2¼ lb) sugar; 3 dl (½ pt) freshly made strong tea; few drops Pektolase; good wine yeast and nutrient; water as in method

If using grape juice instead of sultanas, use 3.5 dl (13 fl oz) hock type and reduce sugar by 125 g (5 oz)

SWEET

1.1 kg (2½ lb) runner beans; 450 g (1 lb) sultanas; 2 medium sized grapefruits and 2 oranges (or equivalent of tinned fruit); 1.125 kg (2½ lb) sugar; 3 dl (½ pt) freshly made strong tea; few drops Pektolase; good wine yeast and nutrient; water as in method

If using grape juice instead of sultanas, use 3.5 dl (13 fl oz) hock type and reduce sugar by 125 g (5 oz)

METHOD

Wash well and prepare beans as for cooking. Proceed as for pea-pod wine on p. 115, adding the strained grapefruit juce at the time when you would add the orange juice.

PARSLEY WINES

Parsley is a herb, but the method fits well into this chapter. Use young fresh parsley and wash it well.

DRY

450 g (1 lb) parsley; 450 g (1 lb) sultanas; 775 g (1¾ lb) sugar; 2 oranges; 1 level 5 ml spoonful citric acid; 3 dl (½ pt) freshly made strong tea; few drops Pektolase; good wine yeast and nutrient; water as in method

If using grape juice instead of sultanas, use 3.5 dl (13 fl oz) rosé or hock type and reduce sugar by 125 g (5 oz)

MEDIUM

550 g (1¼ lb) parsley; 450 g (1 lb) sultanas; 1 kg (2¼ lb) sugar; 2 oranges; 1 level 5 ml spoonful citric acid; 3 dl (½ pt) freshly made strong tea; good wine yeast and nutrient; water as in method

If using grape juice instead of sultanas, use 3.5 dl (13 fl oz) rosé or hock type and reduce sugar by 125 g (5 oz)

SWEET

675 g (1½ lb) parsley; 450 g (1 lb) sultanas; 1.125 kg (2½ lb) sugar; 2 oranges; 1 level 5 ml spoonful citric acid; 3 dl (½ pt) freshly made strong tea; good wine yeast and nutrient; water as in method
If using grape juice instead of sultanas, use 3.5 dl (13 fl oz) hock type and reduce sugar by 125 g (5 oz)

METHOD

Proceed as for pea-pod wine on p. 115.

11
WINES FROM CITRUS FRUITS

Some very excellent wines may be made from citrus fruit and these recipes make for rather better-quality wines than those made from canned citrus fruit or juices.

TANGERINE WINES

12-15 tangerines; 450 g (1 lb) sultanas; 225 g (½ lb) bananas weighed after peeling; 3 dl (½ pt) freshly made strong tea; few drops Pektolase; good wine yeast and nutrient; sugar: for dry use 675 g (1½ lb); for medium use 950 g (2 lb 2 oz); for sweet use 1.050 kg (2 lb 6 oz); water as in method

METHOD

Peel the tangerines and discard the peel, remove pips and then crush the fruits, being careful not to lose any juice. Put them in the fermenting pail. Chop or mince the sultanas and add these to the tangerines. Put the sugar in about 2½ l (4 pt) of hot water, bring slowly to the boil, stirring constantly, and while boiling pour over the fruits and give a thorough stirring. Mash the peeled bananas with a fork and put them in about 1.2 l (2 pt) water in a saucepan larger than you would normally use because they will boil up like milk. Simmer gently with the lid on for twenty minutes, topping up with more water if necessary. Then stir this into the mixture. Add the tea, cover closely, allow to cool to about 18°C (65°F) – lukewarm – and then stir in the yeast and nutrient. Cover the vessel with sheet polythene, tie this down tightly (or fit the lid) and put the mixture in the warm to ferment for five or six days, stirring daily.

Having done this, strain the mixture through three or four thicknesses of muslin, press the pulp as dry as you can, clean the fermenting vessel and return the strained wine to this. Then bring the mixture up to just under 5 l (1 gall) with boiled water that has cooled well. Stir in the Pektolase, cover as before and leave in the warm to ferment for a further ten days. The next step is to pour very carefully into a 5 l (1 gall) jar leaving as much deposit in the pail as you can. If the jar is not filled to where the neck begins, fill to this level with boiled water, then fit a fermentation lock and leave until all fermentation has ceased.

ORANGE WINES

Use thin-skinned oranges.

12-14 oranges; 450 g (1 lb) sultanas; 225 g (½ lb) bananas weighed after peeling; 3 dl (½ pt) freshly made strong tea; few drops Pektolase; good wine yeast and nutrient; sugar: for dry use; 675 g (1½ lb); for medium use 950 g (2 lb 2 oz); for sweet use 1.050 kg (2 lb 6 oz); water as in method

METHOD

Grate the rind off the oranges and set it aside. Halve the oranges, press out all the juice and fleshy parts, remove pips and put the juice and fleshy parts in the fermenting pail with the chopped sultanas. Put the sugar in about 2½ l (4 pt) of hot water, bring slowly to the boil stirring constantly and while boiling, pour over the fruits in the fermenting pail and give a good stirring. Add the grated orange peel.

Mash the peeled bananas with a fork and put them in about 1.2 l (2 pt) of water in a saucepan larger than you would normally use because they boil up like milk. Simmer gently with the lid on for twenty minutes, topping up with more water if necessary. Stir this into the mixture and then add the tea. Allow to cool to about 18°C (65°F) – luke warm – and then stir in the yeast and nutrient. Cover the vessel with sheet polythene, tie this down tightly (or fit the lid) and put the mixture in the warm to ferment for six or seven days stirring daily.

Having done this, strain the mixture through three or four thicknesses of muslin, press the pulp as dry as you can, clean the fermenting vessel and return the strained wine to this. Make up the mixture to not more than 5 l (1 gall) with boiled water that has cooled well, stir in the Pektolase, cover as before and put the wine in the warm to ferment for a further ten days. The next step is to pour carefully into a 5 l (1 gall) jar leaving as much deposit in the pail as you can. If the jar is not filled to where the neck begins, fill to this level with boiled water that has cooled, then fit a fermentation lock and leave until all fermentation has ceased.

GRAPEFRUIT WINES

Best made as dry to medium.

6 large grapefruit; 675 g (1½ lb) sultanas; 3 dl (½ pt) strong tea; few drops Pektolase; good wine yeast and nutrient; sugar: for dry use 550 g (1¼ lb); for medium use 775 g (1¾ lb); and, if you insist upon a sweet wine, use 900 g (2 lb); water as in method

METHOD
Proceed as for tangerine wine on p. 118, ignoring the instructions regarding bananas.

12
FLOWER WINES

In previous works on this subject I have recommended the use of a synthetic must in flower wines as a basic fermentable medium and one which improved these wines a good deal. This is not now available. It is a fact that flowers themselves do not produce good fermentation although we add tannin in the form of tea and acid in the form of citric – two essentials of a good fermentation and of a well-balanced wine. Yeast will of course ferment the sugar, but more than just sugar, acid and tannin are needed for a good wine. Because the synthetic must is no longer available we must revert to an old stand-by that gives the yeast 'something to get its teeth into' and which improves the wines very greatly: raisins or sultanas. Raisins however give their flavour into the wine and in these delicately aromatic wines raisin flavour would be out of place. We must settle for sultanas which give the yeast what it needs and the wine some character and fullness without any flavour, so that the delicate flavours of the flowers come to the fore.

These wines, like wines made from vegetables (Chapter 10), are unique in that their like cannot be found anywhere except where they are made.

Reminders When measuring the amount of flowers required put them in a measuring jug and gently bump the jug on a wooden surface to settle the flowers, petals or florets. Do not press down by hand, otherwise too much may be used; in the case of elderflowers and hawthorn blossom the result would be wines with an overpowering flavour.

The amount of citric acid, together with the citric acid contained in the oranges, has been found to be sufficient for flower wines. However tastes vary and if you feel that a little more is needed, you may always use it.

DANDELION WINES

Gather the flowers on a sunny day, without picking the tiniest piece of stalk. The stalk contains a bitter 'milk' which could find its way into the wine and make it bitter. When gathered, the heads close up, so all you need do is to hold the green calix in one hand and pull off all the petals with the other. This can be done when you get home.

DRY

3 qt dandelion petals(about 1 gall heads); 450 g (1 lb) sultanas; 675 g (1½ lb) sugar; 3 dl (½ pt) freshly made strong tea; 1 level 5 ml spoonful citric acid; 2 oranges; good wine yeast and nutrient; few drops Pektolase; water as in method

MEDIUM

3 qt dandelion petals (about 1 gall heads); 450 g (1 lb) sultanas; 1 kg (2¼ lb) sugar; 3 dl (½ pt) freshly made strong tea; 1 level 5 ml spoonful citric acid; 2 oranges; good wine yeast and nutrient; few drops Pektolase; water as in method

SWEET

4 qt dandelion petals (about 5 qt heads); 450 g (1 lb) sultanas; 1.125 kg (2½ lb) sugar; 3 dl (½ pt) freshly made strong tea; 1 level 5 ml spoonful citric acid; 2 oranges; good wine yeast and nutrient; few drops Pektolase; water as in method

METHOD

Put the flowers in the fermenting vessel with the chopped sultanas, tea, sugar and citric acid and pour on about 4 l (7 pt) of boiling water. Stir well to dissolve the sugar, cover closely and leave to cool to about 18°C (65°F) – lukewarm. Then stir in the yeast nutrient and Pektolase. Grate the orange rind over the mixture. Then halve the oranges, press out the juice, strain it and stir the strained juice into the mixture. Cover with sheet polythene (or fit the lid), tie down tightly with strong string and put the mixture in the warm to ferment for eight or nine days, stirring daily.

The next step is to strain out the solids through three or four thicknesses of muslin and to press as dry as you can. Clean the fermenting pail and return the strained wine to this. Cover as before and leave in the warm to continue fermenting for a further five or six days, or a little longer if fermentation still appears fairly vigorous.

Having done this, pour very carefully into a 5 l (1 gall) jar leaving as much deposit in the pail as you can. Fill the jar to where the neck begins. If not filled to this level, top up with boiled water, then fit a fermentation lock and leave until all fermentation has ceased.

GORSE WINES

Pale golden beauties.

DRY
3 qt gorse flowers; 450 g (1 lb) sultanas; 775 g (1¾ lb) sugar; 3 dl (½ pt) freshly made strong tea; 1 level 5 ml spoonful citric acid; 2 oranges; few drops Pektolase; good wine yeast and nutrient; water as in method

MEDIUM
3½ qt gorse flowers; 450 g (1 lb) sultanas; 1.125 kg (2½ lb) sugar; 3 dl (½ pt) freshly made strong tea; 1 level 5 ml spoonful citric acid; 2 oranges; few drops Pektolase; good wine yeast and nutrient; water as in method

SWEET
1 gall gorse flowers; 450 g (1 lb) sultanas; 1.225 g (2¾ lb) sugar; 3 dl (½ pt) freshly made strong tea; 1 level 5 ml spoonful citric acid; 3 oranges; few drops Pektolase; good wine yeast and nutrient; water as in method

METHOD
Proceed as for dandelion wine on p. 122.

ROSE-PETAL WINES

This wine varies considerably with the varieties of rose-petals used. Try to use as many fragrant sorts as possible. Colour is not important, but the more red varieties used the more attractive the wine will be. If you cannot obtain enough petals at the start, add more during fermentation. The petals should be collected as they are almost ready to drop. Do not make this wine sweet, unless you insist, in which case follow the recipe for medium, but use 1.125 kg (2½ lb) sugar.

DRY
6 pt rose petals; 450 g (1 lb) sultanas; 775 g (1¾ lb) sugar; 3 dl (½ pt) freshly made strong tea; 1 level 5 ml spoonful citric acid; 2 oranges; few drops Pektolase; good wine yeast and nutrient; water as in method

MEDIUM
6-8 pt rose petals; 450 g (1 lb) sultanas; 1.450 g (3¼ lb) sugar; 3 dl (½ pt) freshly made strong tea; 1 level 5 ml spoonful citric acid; 2 oranges; few drops Pektolase; good wine yeast and nutrient; water as in method

METHOD

Proceed as for dandelion wines on p. 122.

If you have to add petals to make up the total during fermentation, extend the fermentation period in the pail a few days longer, but take off or strain out the first lot of petals after eight or nine days.

ELDERFLOWER WINES

Delightfully pungent flavour, but quite strong so few florets are needed. Do not make a sweet elderflower wine unless you insist, in which case use ½ pt more florets and 1.125 kg (2½ lb) sugar. However you may find that a sweet wine lacks flavour; using more florets is not the answer because the pungency of flavour may be a little too strong.

DRY
1 pt elderflowers; 450 g (1 lb) sultanas; 775 g (1¾ lb) sugar; 3 dl (½ pt) freshly made strong tea (or pinch grape tannin if you want a white wine); 1 level 5 ml spoonful citric acid; 2 oranges; few drops Pektolase; good wine yeast and nutrient; water as in method

MEDIUM
As above, but use 1 kg (2¼ lb) sugar.

(124)

METHOD

Proceed as for dandelion wine on p. 122.
If you use grape tannin instead of tea, add when you would the tea.

HAWTHORN BLOSSOM WINES

Another pungently flavoured white wine which is whiter if a pinch of grape tannin is used instead of the tea. Hawthorn blossom wine is not the best when sweet because the sweetness reduces the flavour. Using more blossom produces a rather too strong a flavour. But you can try it if you like using 2 pints blossom and 1.125 kg (2½ lb) sugar.

DRY

1½ pt hawthorn blossom; 450 g (1 lb) sultanas; 775 g (1¾ lb) sugar; 3 dl (½ pt) freshly made strong tea (or pinch grape tannin); 1 level 5 ml spoonful citric acid; 2 oranges; few drops Pektolase; good wine yeast and nutrient; water as in method

MEDIUM

Follow the above recipe, using 1 kg (2¼ lb) sugar.

METHOD

Proceed as for dandelion wine on p. 122, adding the tannin when you would the tea.

13
RHUBARB AS A BASIC INGREDIENT

Rhubarb is a very versatile ingredient that may be used alone – with additives to assist fermentation – or with a variety of other fruits to produce a profusion of recipes for some really outstanding wines. The advantages of rhubarb are that it is cheap, plentiful and has a long season, especially if you happen to grow it yourself as, in my view, anybody with a small garden that gets the sunshine for a few hours a day should do.

The characteristic flavour of rhubarb prevents us imitating commercial products when it is used alone, but blended, as in the recipes, with other fruits a wide variety of wines similar to commercial products can be made.

Wines containing the flavour of rhubarb, however slight this may be in certain finished wines made from the recipes here, are in my view better for being dry to medium. But I am well aware that many people must have their wines sweet regardless, so I include a sweet recipe for each blend of ingredients.

RHUBARB WINES
Resembling rieslings

DRY
900 g (2 lb) rhubarb; 450 g (1 lb) sultanas; 2 grapefruits (or equivalent tinned); 675 g (1½ lb) sugar; 3 dl (½ pt) freshly made strong tea (or pinch grape tannin); few drops Pektolase; good wine yeast and nutrient; water as in method

MEDIUM

900 g (2 lb) rhubarb; 450 g (1 lb) sultanas; 2 grapefruits (or equivalent tinned); 1 kg (2¼ lb) sugar; 3 dl (½ pt) freshly made strong tea; good wine yeast and nutrient; water as in method

SWEET

1.125 kg (2½ lb) rhubarb; 450 g (1 lb) sultanas; 3 grapefruits (or equivalent tinned); 1.125 kg (2½ lb) sugar; 3 dl (½ pt) freshly made strong tea; good wine yeast and nutrient; water as in method

METHOD

Wipe the rhubarb with a damp cloth, cut them into chunks 2.5 cm (1 in) long, being careful not to lose any juice, and then bruise them well with the end of a rolling pin or a similar implement. Put them in the fermenting vessel with the chopped or minced sultanas and add the the grapefruit juice strained free of pips. The fleshy parts can go in. Having done this, pour on about 2½ l (4 pt) of boiling water and give the mixture a good stirring.

Put the sugar in about 1.2 l (2 pt) of water in a saucepan and bring it slowly to the boil, stirring constantly to prevent burning. When the sugar is thoroughly dissolved and the resultant syrup is boiling pour it into the mixture and give another stirring. Cover well and leave to cool to about 18°C (65°F) – lukewarm. Then add the tea, yeast and nutrient. Cover the vessel with sheet polythene and tie this down tightly (or fit the lid). Put the mixture in the warm to ferment for ten days, stirring daily.

The next step is to strain the wine through three or four thicknesses of muslin. Press the pulp as dry as you can, clean the fermenting vessel and return the strained wine to this. Add the Pektolase, cover as before and leave in the warm to ferment for a further five or six days. Do not stir during this time.

Having done this, pour the wine carefully into a 5 l (1 gall) jar, leaving as much deposit in the pail as you can. If the jar is not filled to where the neck begins, fill to this level with boiled water which has been allowed to cool a little. Then fit a fermentation lock and leave until all fermentation has ceased.

WINES INCLUDING RHUBARB

All these should be dry, but many will want them medium to sweet as well – so here goes. Use tea (tannin) and acid only where advised.

1 CLARET TYPE
900 g (2 lb) rhubarb; 900 g (2 lb) tinned blackberries; 225 g (½ lb) sultanas; few drops Pektolase; ¼ pt freshly made strong tea (or pinch grape tannin); good wine yeast and nutrient; sugar: for dry use 900 g (2 lb); for medium use 1.125 kg (2½ lb); for sweet use 1.225 kg (2¾ lb); water as in method

2 ANOTHER CLARET
675 g (1½ lb) rhubarb; 450 g (1 lb) dried currants; ½ level 5 ml spoonful citric acid; few drops Pektolase; 3 dl (½ pt) freshly made strong tea (or pinch grape tannin); good wine yeast and nutrient; sugar: for dry use 775 g (1¾ lb); for medium use 1 kg (2¼ lb); for sweet use 1.125 kg (2½ lb); water as in method

3 ROSÉ STYLE
675 g (1½ lb) rhubarb; 900 g (2 lb) blackcurrants; 225 g (½ lb) sultanas; few drops Pektolase; good wine yeast and nutrient; sugar: for dry use 900 g (2 lb); for medium use 1.125 kg (2½ lb); for sweet use 1.225 kg (2¾ lb); water as in method

4 ANOTHER ROSÉ
900 g (2 lb) rhubarb; 675 g (1½ lb) loganberries (or 900 g (2 lb) tinned); 225 g (½ lb) sultanas; few drops Pektolase; 3 dl (½ pt) freshly made strong tea; good wine yeast and nutrient; sugar: for dry use 775 g (1¾ lb); for medium use 1 kg (2¼ lb); for sweet use 1.125 kg (2½ lb); water as in method

5 A SPECIAL WINE
900 g (2 lb) rhubarb; 450 g (1 lb) dried prunes; 1½ dl (¼ pt) freshly made strong tea (or pinch grape tannin); ½ level 5 ml spoonful citric acid; good wine yeast and nutrient; sugar: for dry use 900 g (2 lb); for medium use 1.125 kg (2½ lb); for sweet use 1.225 kg (2¾ lb); water as in method
Note Soak prunes overnight in enough water to cover, bring to boil slowly and simmer until cooked. Add to rhubarb in fermenting vessel as advised in method for other fruit.

6 LIGHT, FRESH ROSÉ TYPE (dry only)
450 g (1 lb) rhubarb; 225 g (½ lb) sultanas; 450 g (1 lb) tinned prunes; few drops Pektolase; 3 dl (½ pt) freshly made strong tea (or pinch grape tannin); 1 5 ml spoonful citric acid; good wine yeast and nutrient; 900 g (2 lb) sugar; water as in method. The flavour of this one is not strong enough to make a medium or sweet wine, but it is a lovely dry wine.

7 A DELIGHTFUL WHITE WINE (best as a dry wine)
675 g (1½ lb) rhubarb; 450 g (1 lb) sultanas; 900 g (2 lb) gooseberries (or

equivalent canned); 3 dl (½ pt) freshly made strong tea; few drops Pektolase; good wine yeast and nutrient; sugar: for dry use 775 g (1¾ lb); for medium use 1 kg (2¼ lb); for sweet use 1.225 kg (2¾ lb); water as in method
Note The tea will colour the wine slightly, so if you want a really pinky-white wine without a hint of gold in it use ½ level 5 ml spoonful grape tannin.

8 A DELICIOUS CLARET (best when made dry)
1.1 kg (2½ lb) rhubarb; 225 g (½ lb) dried elderberries; 225 g (½ lb) raisins; few drops Pektolase; good wine yeast and nutrient; sugar: for dry use 900 g (2 lb); for medium use 1.125 kg (2½ lb); for sweet use 1.225 kg (2¾ lb); water as in method
Note Thoroughly wash the elderberries in several changes of water. Then put them in about 6 dl (1 pt) of fresh water, bring slowly just to boiling point and then add in the same way other fruits in the method.

METHOD FOR RECIPES 1-8
Before you begin, see notes under recipes 5 and 8 about the preparation of prunes and dried elderberries.

Wipe the rhubarb sticks with a damp cloth, cut them into pieces 2.5 cm (1 in) long, being careful not to lose any juice, and then bruise them well with the end of a rolling pin or a similar implement. Put them in the fermenting pail with the chopped sultanas or raisins (depending on the recipe) and then add all the other ingredients except the yeast, nutrient and Pektolase. Having done this, pour on about 3½ l (6 pt) of boiling water and stir vigorously at once to dissolve the sugar. Do not forget to add the juice of the tinned fruits.

Cover closely and allow the mixture to cool to about 18°C (65°F) – lukewarm – and then stir in the yeast, nutrient and Pektolase. Cover the vessel with sheet polythene and tie this down tightly with thin strong string (or fit the lid). Put in a warm place to ferment for ten days or, where dried elderberries are being used, for only five days. Stir daily.

The next step is to strain out the solids through three or four thicknesses of muslin and to wring out the pulp as dry as you can. Clean the fermenting pail and return the strained wine to this. Cover as before and leave in the warm to continue fermenting for a further four of five days, or ten days where dried elderberries are being used.

Having done this, pour carefully into a 5 l (1 gall) jar leaving as much deposit in the pail as you can. The jar will not be full, so fill to where the neck begins with boiled water that has cooled well, then fit a fermentation lock and leave until all fermentation has ceased.

14
APPLE WINES

Apples, like rhubarb, are a very useful basic ingredient. Combined with a variety of other ingredients they make some excellent wines which could not be obtained any other way.

Apples contain pectin and sometimes a little starch. We shall be adding Pektolase as a matter of course to destroy the pectin which, as we have seen earlier, prevents wines from clearing. So we are assured of a clear wine, provided starch does not give us a problem here. Starch, as we know, also gives a clearing problem. But in these recipes, as in those for wines from vegetables, we add the sugar in two stages. This is in the hope of inducing the yeast to convert the starch to sugar and ferment it out to leave a brilliant wine. But this plan, discussed in chapter 10 'Making Wines with Vegetables', does not always work. So we wait to see if the wine will clear of its own accord – say a week or two after fermentation has ceased. If the wine is not clear by that time, the use of the starch-destroying enzyme, know as fungal amylase, is justified. The amount suggested by the manufacturers is 2.5 g per 25 l (5 gall) of wine. This amount is represented by one capful of the bottle it is supplied in. If you are treating 5 l (1 gall) spread the capful on a piece of clean paper and divide it into four. A quarter will be a trifle more than is required but it will do no harm. If you mix the amount with a little of the wine to be treated and then stir the sample into the bulk, the wine should be clear in a day or so.

Apple wines are always best if two or three varieties are used and this should include a few cooking apples. The following recipe and method for apple wine will make an excellent wine in its own right, so you may go ahead and make it with confidence. Immediately following the method is a list of various fruits that may be added to make a variety of wines still using the basic recipe and method. How to prepare these additional fruits is shown under each fruit and when to add them is shown in the basic method for the apple wine, so everything will be abundantly clear.

APPLE WINES
Basic recipe

3.6 kg (8 lb) mixed apples; 450 g (1 lb) sultanas; 225 g (½ lb) peeled bananas; few drops Pektolase; good wine yeast and nutrient; sugar: for dry use 675 g (1½ lb); for medium use 900 g (2 lb); for sweet use 1 kg (2¼ lb); water as in method

BASIC METHOD

Put 2½ l (4 pt) of water in the fermenting pail (preferably boiled water that has cooled). Crush 1½ Campden fruit-preserving tablets to a fine powder, dissolve this in about an eggcupful of warm water and stir it into the water in the fermenting pail. Thoroughly wash the apples but do not peel them. Core them, cut them up and put them through the coarse plate of the mincer (or through a juice extractor, pulper or whatever you may have). Put the juice and pulp into the water at once. This is to prevent enzymes in the apples causing browning. Chop or mince the sultanas and add these to the rest. Put half the sugar in about 6 dl (1 pt) of hot water, bring slowly to the boil, stirring constantly to prevent burning. While boiling, stir into the mixture. Cover closely and allow the mixture to cool (if not cool already) to about 18°C (65°F) – lukewarm.

Now is the time to add any of the fruits listed, prepared as advised; merely stir them well in. Having done this, add the yeast and nutrient, cover the vessel with sheet polythene, tie it down tightly with thin strong string (or fit the lid) and keep the mixture in the warm to ferment for eight or nine days stirring daily.

The next step is to strain out the solids through three or four thicknesses of muslin. Wring out the pulp as dry as you can, clean the fermenting vessel and return the strained wine to this. Cover as before, while you put the rest of the sugar in about 6 dl (1 pt) of hot water. Bring it slowly to the boil, stirring constantly, and allow to cool well, before stirring it into the wine.

Peel the bananas and discard the skins. Mash the bananas with a fork, put them in about a quart of water (use a saucepan larger than seems necessary because they boil up like milk), bring slowly to the boil and simmer gently with the lid on for twenty minutes. Strain while hot to remove the fluffy residue. Allow the water to cool and then stir it into the wine. Stir in the Pektolase. Cover as before and leave to ferment for a further three or four days.

Having done this, pour carefully into a 5 l (1 gall) jar, leaving as much deposit in the pail as you can. The jar will most likely be full, but if not, fill to where the neck begins with boiled water, then fit a fermentation lock and leave until all fermentation has ceased.

If, when pouring the liquid into the jar, there is a little too much to go in, put what is left into a small bottle, plug the neck with cotton wool and add it to the jar when the yeast has used up more of the sugar. It will largely depend on whether you used additional fruit besides the ingredients in the basic recipe whether or not there is more than the jar can hold.

ADDITIONS TO THE BASIC APPLE RECIPE

If you add any of these, add them when stated in the basic method.

BLACKBERRIES
900 g (2 lb): simmer in as little water as possible until they begin to pulp, allow to cool and then add them.

SLOES
450 g (1 lb): remove stalk, scald them, crush by hand and then add them.

BILBERRIES (Whortleberries)
As for blackberries loganberries – 900 g (2 lb). Cook in as little water as possible until they begin to pulp. Allow to cool and then add them.

ELDERBERRIES
675 g (1½ lb): simmer in as little water as possible until they begin to pulp and then allow to cool before adding them.

DAMSONS
900 g (2 lb): remove stalks, wash them, scald them, crush them by hand and then stir them in.

PLUMS
Must be fully ripe. As for damsons

BLACKCURRANTS
675 g (1½ lb): simmer in as little water as possible until they begin to pulp. Allow to cool and then stir them in.

PRUNES (dried)

450 g (1 lb): soak overnight. Bring to boil and simmer until cooked and in any case long enough to drive off excess water. Allow to cool, break up with a fork and then add them.

Note If you prefer, or if you are not close to wild or garden fruit, you may use tinned fruits instead of the fresh fruit as given. Not all of them are found in tins so you will be limited if you cannot obtain others from the countryside.

You may use a bottle of Ribena or other blackcurrant syrup instead of blackcurrants, but do not use blackcurrant cordial.

15
WINES FROM
CRAB APPLES

Crab apples are grown mainly as ornamental trees and were once found in profusion in large gardens. Today they are often planted on housing estates and are often found growing wild. The apples are quite tiny – and somewhat like bright red or yellow rose hips, but a good deal larger – about twice the weight generally. They are quite astringent to the palate and are therefore useful for making slightly astringent aperitifs. The astringency can, in effect, be regarded as dryness even in a medium sweet wine. This is because the astringency 'shows' through the unfermented sugar.

I have always regarded crab apples as best for making dry wines rather than sweet, but you may make them sweet if you want them that way.

As explained in Chapter 10 'Making Wines with Vegetables', you may use concentrated grape juice instead of the sultanas given in the recipe if you want to. So under each recipe there appears the name of a type of concentrate followed by 'reduce sugar by 125 g (5 oz)'. Bear in mind that if you do not use the sultanas as given in the recipe you will have to increase the amount of sugar in each recipe by 225 g (8 oz) to make up for the sugar contained in them. But because you will be using 3.5 dl (13 fl oz) of concentrate which contains a lot of sugar you will then have to reduce the sugar by 350 g (13 oz). So the difference is 125 g (5 oz) and you therefore reduce the sugar given in the recipe by this amount. Do bear in mind that 13 oz of dry sugar is not the same as 13 fl oz liquid measure.

There are two reasons for choosing 3.5 dl (13 fl oz) of concentrate: the most important is that it is just the right amount for 5 l (1 gall) of wine while allowing for the other ingredients, and because it is just half of the popular 1 kg can. This means that you have the right amount left for a second batch. All these wines are made by the same method which is given at the end of the chapter on p. 138.

PLAIN CRAB WINES
A delightful aperitif when dry

DRY

1.1 kg (2½ lb) crab apples; 2 oranges; 450 g (1 lb) sultanas; few drops Pektolase; good wine yeast and nutrient; 775 g (1¾ lb) sugar; water as in method
If using grape juice instead of sultanas, use 3.5 dl (13 fl oz) hock type and reduce sugar by 125 g (5 oz)

MEDIUM

1.3 kg (3 lb) crab apples; 2 oranges; 450 g (1 lb) sultanas; few drops Pektolase; good wine yeast and nutrient; 1 kg (2¼ lb) sugar; water as in method
If using grape juice instead of sultanas, use 3.5 dl (13 fl oz) hock type and reduce sugar by 125 g (5 oz)

SWEET

1.6 kg (3½ lb) crab apples; 3 oranges; 450 g (1 lb) sultanas; few drops Pektolase; good wine yeast and nutrient; 1.125 kg (2½ lb) sugar; water as in method
If using grape juice instead of sultanas, use 3.5 dl (13 fl oz) hock type and reduce sugar by 125 g (5 oz)

CRAB APPLE AND APRICOT WINES
Delicious as a dry aperitif

DRY

1.1 kg (2½ lb) crab apples; 450 g (1 lb) sultanas; 900 g (2 lb) fresh or tinned apricots; few drops Pektolase; good wine yeast and nutrient; 775 g (1¾ lb) sugar; water as in method
If using grape juice instead of sultanas, use 3.5 dl (13 fl oz) rosé or hock type and reduce sugar by 125 g (5 oz)

MEDIUM

1.1 kg (2½ lb) crab apples; 450 g (1 lb) sultanas; 900 g (2 lb) fresh or tinned apricots; few drops Pektolase; good wine yeast and nutrient; 1 kg (2¼ lb)

(135)

sugar; water as in method

If using grape juice instead of sultanas, use 3.5 dl (13 fl oz) rosé or hock type and reduce sugar by 125 g (5 oz)

SWEET

1.3 kg (3 lb) crab apples; 450 g (1 lb) sultanas; 900 g (2 lb) fresh or tinned apricots; few drops Pektolase; good wine yeast and nutrient; 1.125 kg (2½ lb) sugar; water as in method

If using grape juice instead of sultanas, use 3.5 dl (13 fl oz) rosé or hock type and reduce sugar by 125 g (5 oz)

CRAB APPLE AND PRUNE WINES

A delicious rosé type, best when dry, but you will like it sweet if you like sweet wines.

DRY

1.1 kg (2½ lb) crab apples; 450 g (1 lb) sultanas; 225 g (½ lb) dried prunes or 900 g (2 lb) tinned; few drops Pektolase; good wine yeast and nutrient; 775 g (1¾ lb) sugar; water as in method

If using grape juice instead of sultanas, use 3.5 dl (13 fl oz) rosé type and reduce sugar by 125 g (5 oz)

MEDIUM

1.1 kg (2½ lb) crab apples; 450 g (1 lb) sultanas; 225 g (½ lb) dried prunes or 900 g (2 lb) tinned; few drops Pektolase; good wine yeast and nutrient; 1 kg (2¼ lb) sugar; water as in method

If using grape juice instead of sultanas, use 3.5 dl (13 fl oz) rosé type and reduce sugar by 125 g (5 oz)

SWEET

1.3 kg (3 lb) crab apples; 450 g (1 lb) sultanas; 225 g (½ lb) dried prunes or 900 g (2 lb) tinned; few drops Pektolase; good wine yeast and nutrient; 2½ lb sugar; water as in method

If using grape juice instead of sultanas, use 3.5 dl (13 fl oz) rosé type and reduce sugar by 125 g (5 oz)

CRAB APPLE AND BLACKBERRY WINES

Three delicious wines. Do not use grape juice.

DRY

900 g (2 lb) crab apples; 900 g (2 lb) blackberries; 225 g (½ lb) sultanas; few drops Pektolase; good wine yeast and nutrient; 900 g (2 lb) sugar; water as in method

MEDIUM

900 g (2 lb) crab apples; 1.1 kg (2½ lb) blackberries; 225 g (½ lb) sultanas; few drops Pektolase; good wine yeast and nutrient; 1.125 kg (2½ lb) sugar; water as in method

SWEET

1.1 kg (2½ lb) crab apples; 1.1 kg (2½ lb) blackberries; 225 g (½ lb) sultanas; few drops Pektolase; 1.225 kg (2¾ lb) sugar; water as in method

CRAB APPLE AND LOGANBERRY WINES

Top-class rosé type when dry. May be made medium or sweet.

DRY

900 g (2 lb) crab apples; 450 g (1 lb) sultanas; 900 g (2 lb) fresh or tinned loganberries; few drops Pektolase; good wine yeast and nutrient; 775 g (1¾ lb) sugar; water as in method
If using grape juice instead of sultanas, use 3.5 dl (13 fl oz) rosé type and reduce sugar by 125 g (5 oz)

(137)

MEDIUM

900 g (2 lb) crab apples; 450 g (1 lb) sultanas; 900 g (2 lb) fresh or tinned loganberries; few drops Pektolase; good wine yeast and nutrient; 1 kg (2¼ lb) sugar; water as in method

If using grape juice instead of sultanas, use 3.5 dl (13 fl oz) rosé type and reduce sugar by 125 g (5 oz)

SWEET

1.1 kg (2½ lb) crab apples; 450 g (1 lb) sultanas; 900 g (2 lb) fresh or tinned loganberries; few drops Pektolase; good wine yeast and nutrient; 1.125 kg (2½ lb) sugar; water as in method

If using grape juice instead of sultanas, use 3.5 dl (13 fl oz) rosé type and reduce sugar by 125 g (5 oz)

METHOD FOR CRAB APPLE WINES

PREPARING THE FRUIT

Crab apples: remove stalks, wash thoroughly, then chop or mince.

Sultanas: chop or mince.

Oranges   (where used): grate the peel onto the mixture, then halve the oranges, press out the juice, strain it free of pips and fleshy parts, and stir in.

Prunes: soak overnight in enough water to cover, bring slowly to the boil and simmer until tender. Break up with a fork and then add to mixture. Or merely pour the tinned prunes into the mixture.

Apricots: peel, halve, remove stones, chop up without losing any juice, or pour tinned apricots straight into mixture.

Blackberries: remove stalks, wash and then add to mixture.

Loganberries: remove stalks, wash and then add or pour the tinned logan-berries straight into mixture.

Choose your recipe and put the ingredients aside. Put 2½ l (4 pt) of water (preferably boiled and cooled) in the fermenting pail. Crush one Campden fruit-preserving tablet to a fine powder, dissolve this in about an eggcupful of warm water and stir it into the water in the fermenting vessel. Prepare the crab apples as advised and put them in the water at once as you prepare them. Then stir in all the other ingredients except the sugar, yeast, nutrient and Pektolase.

Put the sugar in 1.2 l (2 pt) hot water in a saucepan, bring it slowly to the boil stirring constantly to prevent burning and boil gently for a minute or two. Allow this to cool well, then stir it into the mixture. Give the whole a thorough stirring and then add the yeast, nutrient and Pektolase. Cover the vessel with sheet polythene and tie this down tightly (or fit the lid) and ferment in the warm for six days, stirring daily and covering again at once.

Having done this, strain the mixture through three or four thicknesses of muslin, wring out the pulp as dry as you can, clean the fermenting vessel and return the strained wine to it. Cover as before and keep it in the warm for a further seven or eight days or until the first vigorous fermentation shows signs of slowing. Then pour very carefully into a 5 l (1 gall) jar, leaving as much deposit in the pail as you can. Fill the jar to where the neck begins with boiled water that has cooled somewhat, then fit a fermentation lock and leave in the warm until all fermentation has ceased.

16
SPECIAL ADDITIVES

Mainly for Experienced Wine-Makers

In various recipes in this book a certain amount of sultanas, raisins or bananas is included. Where these ingredients appear they must be used because they form part of the recipe and therefore are important to the finished wine.

But in many recipes, notably those for making wines from wild and garden fruits in Chapters 8 and 9, no mention of these fruits is given. This is because to mention them in recipes and then add in the method, 'If using so and so, leave out this and that, and add whatever is suggested,' would have you tied up in knots in no time, so that you would throw the book out of the window and go out to buy something easier to get on with.

But the fact remains that experience is teaching us all (and I am still learning even after thirty-five years of winemaking) that additional ingredients can and do improve quality, add to all-round fullness and improve or alter slightly the flavour of the main ingredient, while allowing it to predominate as it should.

Naturally, newcomers to the hobby will leave well alone and use the recipes as they are, but those with a good deal of experience who would not find handling rather a lot of different ingredients any problem will be ready to have a go. They will know in advance whether the wines they have been making would be improved or not, and whether the recipes they have been using are producing wines good enough for them. So these special additives are what might be called optional extras and some important points about them should be borne in mind. However, I must repeat that where the ingredients form part of a recipe they must be used.

The important points about these optional extras vary with each, except that all dried fruit, currants, raisins, sultanas and dates contain approximately 50% sugar. Therefore, if 450 g (1 lb) of these are added to a recipe that does not include them in the list of ingredients the amount of sugar would have to be reduced by 225 g (½ lb).

Raisins give their flavour into the wine and add a certain amount of vinosity, often an elusive quality in many home-made wines. But not everybody likes the flavour of raisins. They also add a certain amount of body. 450 g (1 lb) raisins equals approximately 1.8 kg (4 lb) grapes. Prepare by chopping finely or mincing and add at a time when they will be sterilized either by the sulphite solution as used in some methods or by the the boiling water or sugar syrup.

Currants also give their flavour into the wine; this is far more marked than with raisins. They should only be used when a red wine is being made. Prepare by chopping finely and add at a time when they will be sterilized either by the sulphite solution as used in some methods or by the boiling water or sugar syrup.

Sultanas give no flavour to alter that of the main ingredient and are therefore ideal where no additional flavour is wanted in the background. They add body and assist fermentation. 450 g (1 lb) of sultanas equals 1.8 kg (4 lb) of grapes. Add at the time advised for raisins. Prepare by chopping.

Dates give a very slight flavour to the wine which is often unnoticed by many wine-makers, although an experienced palate quickly detects that they have been used. Prepare by stoning and halving or chopping. Add at the time advised for raisins.

Figs are not an advised addition to any fruit wine. They may be used in rather small quantities – say 225 g (½ lb) per 5 l (1 gall) of wine – in root wines. Always bear in mind that figs have slight laxative properties when used in small quantities. Prepare by chopping and add at the time advised for raisins.

Bananas are the most recent addition to the wine-maker's lists of ingredients. They add a good deal of body without giving any noticeable flavour or colour into the wine. There are several ways of preparing them and some people use the skins as well after chopping them up. Many hobbyists use them when they are so overripe that the skins have turned black. The sugar content is highest at this stage. I don't like using the chopped skins and I am not fond of using them when black, but I do use them fully ripe.

Normally 225-450 g (½-1 lb) of skinned bananas is an ample addition and 450 g (1 lb) contains roughly 150 g (6 oz) of sugar.

My method of preparing bananas is to skin them, mash them with a fork and put them in about a 1.2 l (2 pt) of water. I then bring them to the boil and simmer for ten minutes. The mixture is then strained and the strained liquor is poured into the prepared must. When boiling I use a saucepan about twice the size normally required because bananas boil up like milk.

Note that 450 g (1 lb) of skinned bananas requires 1.2 l (2 pt), while 225 g (½ lb) would need 6 dl (1 pt). When using bananas where they are not called for in the recipe add them before the direction to make the mixture up to 5 l (1 gall), or whatever amount is given in the method you are using.

Part II
BEER-MAKING

17
WHY MAKE YOUR
OWN BEER?

For several years now there have appeared at regular intervals complaints in the press by licensed victuallers that home-brewers are taking away their trade and that we should be heavily taxed. Evidence this that our beers must be good otherwise we would soon hurry round to the local to buy a 'decent' pint. If publicans are worried about us making our own beer they should get onto the necks of the breweries to make the kind of beer we like instead of what is most economical and most profitable to them. The main complaint about modern pub beer is that it is thin and weak. This is easy to understand when you consider that it is malt which gives beer its flavour and body (and which *should* give it its alcohol content via the process of fermentation) and that breweries are now using sugar to produce some of the alcohol instead of more malt. In reducing the amount of malt, they automatically reduce flavour and body. So it is only their fault if sales go down and people make their own.

I note that in 1973 one particular brewery group made a profit of £57 million (£1 million a week and a bit to spare) and because they were disappointed with this, having expected £60 million they upped the price by 1p per pint; then they wonder why we are making our own. I have no figures for 1974 or 1975. Like a good many other people, I can well remember good, wholesome, full-flavoured, full-strength beer at 4d a pint (that is three pints for today's 5p piece). And I imagine that there are a good few people still alive who can remember even better beer at a 1d per pint (that is twelve pints for 5p). And they say we live in a dream world today! With commercial beers at anything from 25p to 30p a pint it is no wonder that so many millions are making their own at around 30p per gallon, or even less depending on the materials you use.

But it is not only the price of the stuff that bothers most drinkers. The fact is that there are only one or two beers on the market today that are drunk on their own. At every bar no matter where you go you hear orders for mixtures of two beers because neither taken alone is what the drinker wants. The mixture may be for half bottled and half draught beer – mild and bitter, light and bitter, light and Diamond, brown and mild, stout and mild, stout and brown, Guinness and mild; even that much overrated beer, the lager, must have lime to bolster it. Yet I can remember when no one would have thought of mixing their beers because the one was really worth having as it was.

It is a fact that in an hour or so of your spare time once a week enough beer can be made to last an average drinker a fortnight. A 20 l (4 gall) lot may be made in any kitchen and it takes only a moment or two to assess how long thirty-two pints of the best will last.

Home-made beer is cheap, as has already been pointed out, but this does not mean that it is poor when compared with commercial products. On the contrary, many ales, stouts and such like bought over the bar leave a lot to be desired. Once you have the easily-acquired skill you can make yours better than the stuff now costing more than it is worth. And you can learn by simple experiment how to make beers of all sorts which will really suit you rather than having to acquire the taste for some commercial product that has come your way owing to the merging of two brewery groups. The skill in making beers comes in learning how to make the very kind of beer you have been looking for. You may therefore have to make several lots before you are able to say that 'this' is just what you have been looking for and that the recipe you used is the one for you.

This is how skill in home wine-making is acquired. Too many novice wine-makers make a batch of wine with fruit that has become available without giving a thought to what the wine will be like or whether they will like it or not. The fact that it is wine is all that seems to bother them. This sort of person would go to a wine merchant for a bottle of wine with not the faintest idea of what they wanted apart from it being a bottle of wine. No person with any sense would go into a pub not knowing what he wanted. Clearly the home-brewer must have a pretty good idea of what he wants before he begins and then choose the recipe most likely to produce it. If he does this he will very soon succeed at what must be one of the most interesting and rewarding home hobbies there can be.

No licence is needed today and although this is an absolute boon that will make home-brewing as popular as home wine-making (there are more than a million wine-makers in Britain alone) some operators who have been making beers without a licence for as long as they can remember confess that now they are not breaking the law half the fun has been knocked out of it for them. It would seem that the beer was just that much better because in making it they were breaking the law. I suppose there is something in that, for as a child I remember that apples pinched from other people's orchards always tasted better than our own.

(146)

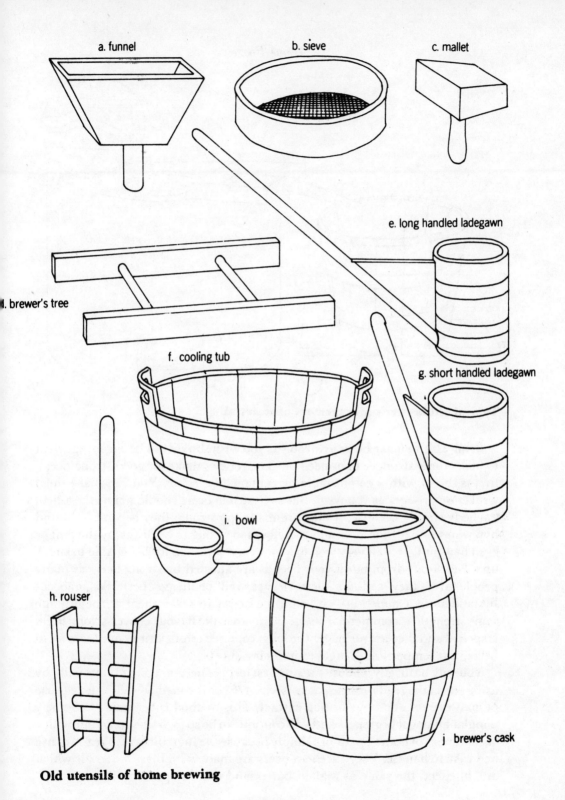

a. funnel

b. sieve

c. mallet

e. long handled ladegawn

d. brewer's tree

f. cooling tub

g. short handled ladegawn

i. bowl

h. rouser

j. brewer's cask

Old utensils of home brewing

(147)

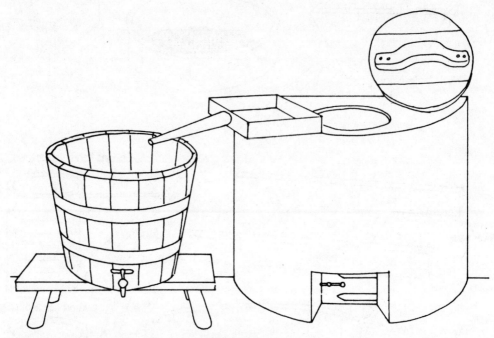

Typical old brewer's arrangement of material

Being able to make beers as strong as you wish should not be encouragement to make them stronger than need be. The recipes make for good strong beers, that is, beers with a comfortable percentage of alcohol. You can make them weaker or stronger as you wish. But over-strong beers should not be the aim of anybody simply because, if they are made too strong, they become malt and hop wines rather than beer and therefore too strong to be drunk by the pint or even half-pint. It is all very well to acquire a reputation for being able to knock up a knock-out drop, but if your friends are affected by strong beers as many people are – they roll up their sleeves and challenge perfectly innocent bystanders to a punch-up – it would be better to make them at roughly the same strength as commercial beers. In any case the flavour of over-strong beers is spoiled and they are no longer the long, cool, refreshing drinks one looks for in beers, but temper and hangover-inducing shorts.

You will, naturally, choose the simplest form of beer-making to start with, by using one of the ready-to-use packs (see p. 176) or the method calling for the use of malt extract and hops or hop extract. This method is becoming extremely popular amongst beginners and will continue to be so for a very long time with a vast number of home-operators simply because the ingredients are ready to use and easy to handle. Very excellent beers are made with these materials which are, in effect, the same as malted barley and dried hops.

Why Make Your Own Beer?

However the more ambitious will want to use grain malt (malted barley) and dried hops, as the commercial brewer does. For this reason, recipes for using either type of ingredients are included, some calling for malt extract and hops extract, others for grain malt and dried hops. Using grain malt (malted barley) and dried hops does make for better beers, but is a little more expensive, slightly more complicated and a little more time-consuming. However the expense – the little there is – should not bar you from going in for making the best possible beers.

Years ago home wine-makers put up with all sorts of disappointing liquors from all sorts of unsuitable fruits and yeast and fermented them in anything but a fire bucket. Today they are a fastidious lot insisting on the best ingredients, the best yeast and the most suitable utensils – and so they should. The result of this new outlook has been the complete transformation of the nature and quality of home-made wines. Years ago hardly any home-made wine was worth drinking; yet today they are absolutely first-class products easily on a par with the best commercial wines.

So let us do as home wine-makers have done and learn to make beers as good as those turned out by famous breweries.

18
BEER-MAKING:
BEFORE WE BEGIN

Ales, beers and stouts are easy to make provided you understand not only why you are working in one particular way, but also why you must work in this way if you want the best results.

There are many methods for making every sort of alcoholic drink; some are good methods ensuring the top-most quality results, while others are so anti-quated and slipshod as to be quite comical. Others are half-way between the two. For far too long too many people have been following methods that can only result in disappointment. The methods here ensure success provided you know what you want before you begin. In saying this, I mean that you should have a good idea of what you want and then set out to make it as near to this as you can expect at a first attempt.

In wine-making we choose to make the wines sweet, medium or dry; light, medium or heavy. Naturally if the beginner wine-maker dislikes dry wines and unwittingly makes them at first attempt, it stands to reason that he will be disappointed. But if he had known what he was about he would have known he was making a dry wine and could have avoided what was to him a calamity because as a beginner he would not necessarily know how to rectify the fault when he had finished. It takes a little time and a few experiments before you can expect to turn out something exactly as you want it. And when you have done this, the experience gained, together with a bit of commonsense, will show you how to improve your product so that it quickly becomes the main and favourite drink of yourself and your friends.

Too many people chuckle apologetically when offering 'a little drop of something I made myself'. Heaven knows why, for it is those who feel they have something to apologize for who turn out the best stuff. Hundreds of times and all over the country I have had people offer me home-made wines, beers, ciders and meads as if they were offering me diluted strychnine and were apologizing for the suffering to come. Mostly they were top-rate wines and beers. It seems to

(150)

me that someone thinks just because he made it it can't be much good. This attitude has its good points because a man like that is clearly anxious to improve his product. But provided he is satisfied I can see no reason for striving to improve it beyond improving it to suit himself even more. After all, as experienced operators will agree, striving to improve can be overdone to such an extent that the end product bears no resemblance to the original. The 'improved' product is then no longer what it was and the operator is disappointed.

The aim should be to find in as few experiments as possible the recipe which gives the results nearest your special liking and then vary slightly the ingredients in future brews. This can be done quite simply by increasing slightly the amount of 'this' and perhaps reducing slightly the amount of 'that' until you produce precisely what you are after.

Altering the amounts of ingredients may not be necessary, for you might well hit the alcoholic nail on the head first time – and I hope you do. Either way you will get a lot of pleasure for a comparatively small outlay, for if your first attempts are not all you hope for you will realize at once that you are onto a good thing, because before long your own brew at 4p or 5p a pint will be as good as your favourite commercial product at 30p a pint.

Commercial Brewing

It stands to reason that if we want good beers we must follow as closely as possible the methods used by those who know how to make them best of all – the commercial brewers. Obviously we cannot possible follow the commercial brewer through every process from growing the barley and hops to bottling the finished product, with gigantic machines handling two or three hundred bottles a minute. Nevertheless we can follow him most of the way.

Firstly we can by-pass two of the most highly-skilled operations by buying quite cheaply ready-to-use ingredients, the very same materials as used by the commercial brewer. Thereafter we can follow him very closely indeed. In fact we might well be very tiny miniatures of the great man himself. There might seem to be no need here for a lengthy discourse on some of the technicalities of commercial brewing. But there is. Anybody can make good beers, but I believe that if the whole process is understood you will be able to see how closely you are following 'the great man himself' and the importance of the simple methods you will be using. The highly technical processes which go on naturally and unseen during these processes without you having much to do with them will be discussed later on.

Beer-making is a natural process, apart from the boiling which is necessary if wild yeasts and bacteria are to be prevented from spoiling the finished product. The changes that take place in the ingredients are natural changes; all we need do is to start them off. Boiling halts these changes and destroys the causes of spoiled beers. Adding yeast merely starts the processes in a liquor freed of the enemies of successful brewing.

The art in commercial brewing is in selecting the materials best suited to the types and varieties of ales and beers turned out by each particular brewer. Any drinker worth his salt will have a wide knowledge of the various ales, beers and stouts available in the houses of the various brewers. The fact that each differs is the result of careful blending of ingredients.

Quality is most important. Brewery groups grow their own barley and hops and harvest and process them according to their needs or select the best from overseas. The body in beer comes from malt obtained from selected barley; hops add flavour, 'tang' and bitterness where this is required and, of course, preservative properties. Yeast in itself adds nothing to beers, yet without it beer would not 'happen'. The action of yeast on sugar in the wort (prepared liquor) produces alcohol, without which the wort would remain wort and never become beer. Sugar is essential if the yeast is to produce alcohol (this point is covered in more detail in the practical section). Invert sugar is used in all breweries, not because it contributes flavour or any effective properties to the finished product, but because it is more readily fermentable than other sugars.

Barley is grown extensively in this country and very often the finest barley in the world is produced here. The quality naturally depends on soil conditions and the weather, the latter being, as we all know well enough, somewhat unpredictable. For this reason a good deal of barley is imported from areas where the climate is more reliable and better suited to growing the very best regularly each season to offset the poor quality sometimes produced here. Thus the commercial brewer might well use barley from Egypt, California, Canada and perhaps India, as well as from Europe and the UK. Barley is simply a seed and contains within its husk, like all seed, the germ of new life with a plentiful supply of food for the young plant.

Barley and malted barley appear identical. Barley is hard, so hard that the miller uses stone to grind it. Malted barley on the other hand is easily cracked with the teeth to exude the soft sweetness which is malt. Malting barley is a highly skilled operation by-passed by amateurs who buy ready malted barley or malt extract. In malting barley the maltster brings about artificial growing conditions so that the seed reacts as if it had been sown in soil. These growing conditions are stopped when the maximum yield of malt can be expected. Firstly the barley is heaped and watered until germination takes place and growth begins. The maltster then spreads the barley on the malting floor and never takes his eyes off it, as it were. Warmth and moisture encourage growth of the shoot within the husk and also bring about digestive ferments which cause starches and other substances to change into malt. When the young shoot still

within the husk is about three-quarters along the seed, the maximum malt yield
is reached. At this stage further growth is halted by drying or lightly cooking in
a kiln. Thus the all-important malt is kept within the husk. The mass of rootlets
is then removed and the malted barley, or malt as it is now called, is stored for
use as required.

The fuller-flavoured, darker-coloured malts are obtained by higher temperatures than those destined for pale ales which are of the palest colour. Crystal
malt is produced by gas-oven treatment. Some malts are roasted while others,
brown malts in particular, are produced in wood-burning kilns. Using one malt
alone or blending two or more in the mash tun is the skill by which the brewer
produces the beers for which he is famed. And it is here, by experiment, that the
home-brewer can turn out something quite remarkable once he has gained a
little experience from using the simple recipes and methods detailed in the
following chapters.

Hops were once described as a noxious weed and outlawed by royal decree,
but without them beers as we know them today would not exist. They are easy
to grow; indeed, my grandfather used to grow them in the same manner as
runner beans. Many country pubs are festooned with hops during the season; it
is from such as these that home wine-makers on a visit to the country pinch a
few for adding to wines which benefit from the addition of a hop or two. The
fully-grown, pale-green hop bears some resemblance to a pine cone except that
it is less tapered and paper-soft instead of woody-hard. Take a handful of
freshly-picked hops and the palms immediately become sticky or tacky. This is
because essential oils and resins have developed in the cone, and it is at this
stage, when the cone is 'ripe', that the hops are gathered, for it is now that the
full flavour is reached.

The drying of hops is a skilled craft. The hops are spread over the cloth-
covered porous floor of the drying kiln through which warm air is passed until
sufficient moisture has been removed to ensure that hops keep well. If too dry
the flavour is spoiled; if not dry enough they could turn mouldy on storing.
When suitably dry the hops are packed by presses and stored until required for
use.

The first operation in commercial brewing is the milling of the malted barley.
As with drying hops and malting the barley, skill is required if the best results
are to be obtained. The malted barley is milled so that it is hardly more than
cracked. From the mill the malted crushed barley or 'grist' is conveyed to the
mash tuns (our mash tun will be a 10 l (2 gall) polythene pail, as we shall see
later on). The mash tuns of the brewery are enormous copper-domed vessels,
often holding many thousands of gallons. It is in these that the first great
changes take place. The malt is fed into these and mixed with water – from now
on called 'liquor' simply because in the brewery there is no such thing as water

except the stuff they wash the floors with. Brewery liquor, then, and malt form the wort in the mash tun. This is brought to and maintained at a temperature suited to the particular enzyme whose action is required to take place first. The temperature is then increased until the brewer is satisfied that the changes brought about by the various enzymes are complete. At this stage the wort is boiled. As soon as the malt is put in the mash tun and wetted, the process halted in the malting kiln recommences. Starch is converted to sugars by digestive ferments or by the enzyme action just mentioned. Temperature control during this stage is essential because certain enzymes work (bring about their changes) at temperatures that would destroy others. Underheating would merely leave certain enzymes inactive so that the desired changes would not take place, or only partly take place. Complete change by enzyme action is necessary if good beers are to be produced.

Conversion and extraction of flavours and other essentials take place in the mash tun. When the wort has been run off the near-spent grain into the coppers for boiling, more hot brewery liquor (not water) is sprayed over the grain until the brewer is satisfied that he has obtained all the goodness he can get. This operation is called sparging.

Next comes boiling. From the mash tuns the wort is run into coppers and boiled with hops. It is during this boiling that the character of the beer is 'fixed' (or decided) and the enzymes which bring about the desired changes in the mash tun are destroyed. Boiling is necessary not only to halt the enzyme action but also to destroy wild yeasts and bacteria by sterilizing. Wild yeasts and bacteria cause spoilage ferments, as in wine-making.

After boiling, the wort is cooled by refrigerating machinery to about 15°C (60°F). At this stage yeast is 'pitched' into the wort; and now the great transformation from murky, flat wort to bright, foaming beer begins. This is known as fermentation, as in wine-making.

A few hops are added during the latter stages of fermentation to add extra tang and preservative properties as some of these will have been lost during boiling.

Varieties of Beer

Whether it be ale, lager, stout, old ale, pale ale or just beer from the barrel it is all beer. But this has not always been so. For centuries 'unhopped' beer (that is, beer made without hops) was known as ale. Only beer made with hops was known as beer. However as time went on hops found their way into all beers whether they were known as ales, beers, stouts or what have you. The real difference between the various beers comes in the treatment of the malted barley and the amount used in the various beers and in the amount of hops used in each. Bitter ale is made with more hops than other beers and the malt used is of the highest-quality pale variety. Light ales are a weaker version of pale ale. Mild ale – the popular draught beer – is made with darker malt. Stouts are made from the darker malts with some roasted malt.

It will be seen that by blending the various malts and by increasing or reducing the amount of hops a wide variety of beers can be made from the two basic materials, malt and hops. The home-brewer has only to use his imagination and his palate to decide on how to alter slightly the amount of an ingredient to produce a beer that will be the envy of his friends. Careful blending of light and dark malts and increasing or reducing the amount of hops used will show readily enough in the variety of beer produced how each may be altered a little more until the operator has designed a recipe for beer that will be the only one for him forever more.

My urging you to experiment does not suggest that you will be disappointed in your first effort. Indeed you will most likely be delighted. I make the suggestion of experimenting in case amongst the many recipes there is not one that suits your palate – but I'm willing to bet there is.

The polythene dustbin is ideal for fermenting brews of 35-50 l (7-10 galls). If this cannot be kept in the warm, a thermostatically controlled heater may be used as in wine-making. All that is necessary is to cut a small slot in the rim of the bin to accommodate the electric head. The thermostat and heater unit may then lie on the bottom.

Utensils

The type and size of utensils will depend to a large extent on the volume of beer being made, and it stands to reason that no one is going to start off a 50 l (10 gall) or 100 l (20 gall) batch at their first shot. The Burco boiler can be used for all operations and this is described in the section on mashing (p. 161).

Another suitable vessel for mashing and sparging and boiling as well as fermenting at a warm temperature is the Bruheat boiler. Unfortunately this does not have a lift-out basket like the Burco boiler. This means that after sparging and when all the wort has been run off, the Bruheat boiler must be cleaned, the wort returned and the process carried on from there. This one holds just over 25 l (5 gall) so would be ideal for boiling a 20 l (4 gall) batch or a smaller one. If you use this boiler make sure your mash is not stodgy. Rather it should be in a watery state.

When you can do so much with one vessel it seems a waste of money to invest in three or four. But much depends on your outlook and the proposed extent of your brewing. Smaller plain boilers, to hold say 10 l (2 gall) can be used for

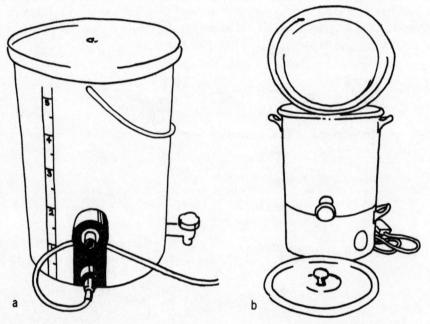

a   b

Boilers
a   The Bruheat Boiler. An excellent and sensitive thermostatically controlled mash-tun/boiler/fermentation vessel in one. As the mash is in contact with the kettle-like element, it is best if the mash is not too stodgy. The sparged and drawn-off wort is returned after cleaning for boiling with the hops, after which the vessel may be used to ferment the beer. It holds just over 25 l (5 galls) which makes it suitable for boiling a 20 l (4 galls) brew.
b   The Burco Boiler. A thermostatically controlled mash-tun/boiler/fermentation vessel. Mashing is simple and the spent grains are retained in the lift-out mesh basket.

See also utensils for wine-making for boilers suitable for boiling small amounts of wort or worts prepared from malt extracts.

small batches. In this case the mashing can be done in a fermenting pail with a thermostatically-controlled heater. The mash is then best kept in suspension in a coarse cloth bag suspended inside the pail. If such a pail has no tap sparging and running off the wort can be done as described under the illustration. If it has a tap the wort can be run off into the boiler while sparging is being carried out.

When a small boiler is used and the amount of beer being made is more than the boiler will hold (leaving one-third empty to allow for boiling up), the amount may be made up with boiled cooled water after boiling which will bring down the temperature quite quickly. This is not quite such good practical brewing as boiling as near as possible the correct amount of wort to the amount of beer you are making, although it does have its advantages where expense is a consideration. However it can prove false economy because sooner or later it is almost certain that you will want to make larger amounts of beer when larger utensils will be needed.

The utensils shown in the various illustrations, in addition to a brewer's thermometer and a specific gravity hydrometer are all that is required.

Draught or Bottled?

The choice is yours. But do take my advice and use a pressure barrel with the appropriate CO_2 cylinder to 'push' out your beer and I am sure that you will be far happier with your draught beer. Bottling large amounts is quite a chore. When you bottle 25 l (5 gall) of wine you obtain around thirty bottles. In normal circumstances, if you are not entertaining, one bottle of wine may last an evening or even longer. So if you use three a week those thirty bottles will last ten weeks. But how long do thirty bottles of beer last? Not long! And with all that washing and sterilizing and corking (capping) and labelling, I can see that draught beers are going to gain popularity once more. Bottled commercial beers gained popularity because of the poorness of commercial draught beers. But this is not the case with home-brewed beers when you are fully experienced. With home-made wine, where goodly amounts are used at one sitting, the 2½ l (4 pt) jar is often opened to avoid the chore of bottling, and if there happens to be a party then the 5 l (1 gall) jar comes into its own, rather than having to open six bottles, then wash, sterilize, fill, label, cork and seal them. So it is with beer. Far easier to use a pressure barrel and draw off the pints or half pints as they are needed, being assured that the CO_2 gas injected into the barrel will keep the remainder of the beer safe and in good heart until it is needed – which may not be long!

It is difficult to recommend one pressure barrel as against another, because all have their virtues and few their drawbacks. It is more often than not simply a case of the one which the operator prefers. Sparklets pressure barrel is excel-

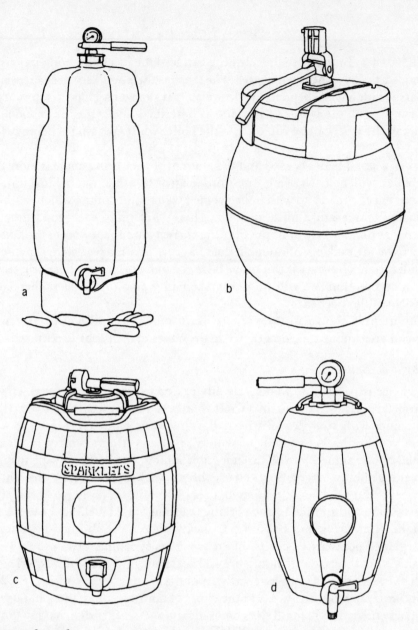

Pressure barrels

a The Brukeg 27½ l (5½ galls) pressure container for all beers. Very strong with moulded hand grips. Marked in gallons and litres and sufficiently transparent for you to see the level of your beer.

b The Eurokeg, fitted with 'Sparklets' bulb dispenser. Ideal for the brewer of smaller amounts of beer, as it ensures that the last pint comes out as fresh as the first.

c The popular 'Sparklets' pressure barrel. As with all other pressure barrels, it is supplied with CO_2 gas injector.

d Another excellent pressure barrel from Homebrews.

(158)

lent. So is the one issued by Hambleton Bard Ltd which has a system whereby you can operate more than one barrel at a time. Brukegs, marketed by Home Brews, is another good one. Eurokegs are designed in various sizes to suit all types of beer-makers; the chap wanting to make 5 or 10 l (1 or 2 gall) at a time and drink it slowly can be assured that his beer will keep well if he only has a couple of half pints a night – which is a good deal less than I have. Naturally full directions are supplied with each pressure barrel and these are quite simple to follow. At most major wine and beer supply shops there is a qualified assistant to explain and demonstrate whichever you choose. There is no need for me to go into details of each, and in any case there are so many makes now that it is impossible to have experience with all of them. But I will say that the Eurokegs have become a firm favourite with very many home-brewers.

Brewers' Jargon

Adjuncts   Materials besides malt, such as wheat, rice or maize, used in brewing to assist in the production of a full-bodied beer.

Bottom-fermenting yeast   This yeast settles to the bottom of the fermenting vessel. It is used mainly on the continent but sometimes in home-brewing.

Caramel   Burnt sugar used for darkening beers where required

Condition   The state of beer brought about by the gas given off by the priming sugar and (more recently) the state brought about by injected gas.

Crushed or cracked barley   Barley prepared for brewing.

Dextrins   Essential substances found in the wort during mashing.

Diastase   An enzyme in grain barley which converts starches to fermentable sugars.

Finings   Isinglass or other clarifiers such as Irish moss.

Grist   Malted barley and adjuncts prepared for the mash tun.

Lactose   Unfermentable milk sugar used to sweeten beers such as brown ales or stouts.

Malt   Malted barley or malt still within the grain.

Malt extract   Malt extracted from the grain and obtainable in syrup form or as a powder.

Mash   Grist (see above) in the mash tun.

Mashing   The process by which the malt and adjuncts are steeped in water and held at a certain temperature to allow enzymes to convert the starches to fermentable sugars.

Mash tun   In our case usually a two-gallon polythene pail.

Pitching   Adding the yeast.

Priming   Adding sugar to fully-fermented beer to bring about secondary fermentation within the bottles.

Priming sugar   Sugar used for priming.

Sparging   The act of washing the spent grain free of fermentable sugar adhering to them and bringing the amount of wort up to the required amount.

Specific gravity   As in wine-making (see p. 57).

Top-fermenting yeast   The popular yeast that forms a knobbly eiderdown on vigorously fermenting beer.

Wort   Mixture free of all solids ready for boiling; also called wort while boiling and during fermentation.

19
THE BEER-MAKING OPERATION

Mashing

Mashing is a natural process. All we have to do is to create the conditions in the mash (cracked grain malts) and water (brewery liquor) which allow the enzymes to break down the starches into fermentable sugars. Diastase is the enzyme which converts the starch into dextrins and maltose. The yeast at a later stage ferments the maltose very rapidly, whereas the dextrins are not so readily fermentable. Temperature during mashing is important if the natural changes brought about by enzyme action are to be satisfactory. Normally a temperature of 65°C (150°F) is quite suitable, but it will not matter if this varies by one degree either side and with modern thermostatically-controlled mash tuns this is quite easy to maintain. After the starch test (see p. 162) shows that all starch has been converted it will not matter if the temperature falls to as low as 55°C (130°F) if, for example, you want to leave the mash to look after itself while you go shopping or even overnight. However leaving overnight is not recommended if you cannot attend to it first thing in the morning, and by this I mean that it is not wise to leave it for longer than eight hours. Whether it should be left as long as this depends largely upon the mash itself. Thick or stodgy mashes should not be left too long, though they do take longer to complete than thinner or dilute mashes. A porridgy mash is quite suitable for enzyme action during the first hour or hour and a half or until starch conversion is complete, but after that it is wise to dilute with hot water, being careful not to raise the temperature above 65°C (150°F). Normally a pint or a quart of water is sufficient and if this is at, say, 65°C (150°F) then it cannot raise the temperature of the mash higher than this.

It is appreciated that the water mixed with the grains in the mash tun should be about 75°C (170°F), but if this is mixed in fairly slowly, stirring the grains to ensure thorough dispersal, the extra heat is unlikely to harm the delicate enzymes. The idea in using water at 75°C (170°F) is that the water is cooled to

(161)

65°C (150°F) as the malts are stirred in. I give the figure 65°C (150°F) which is the usual mashing temperature but it can be minus or plus one degree quite safely. It is essential that the grains be thoroughly dispersed throughout, otherwise there may be small areas or clumps of grains not sufficiently wetted. Once the grains have been stirred in it is important to maintain the temperature at 65°C (150°F) or the figure quoted in the recipe if this is different.

The amount of water to preheat in the boiler ready for the malts to be stirred in is about 2 l (3½ pt) for each 450 g (1 lb) of 'goods' (goods are the ingredients in the recipes – the various malts and flakes – excluding the hops and yeast). So if the total weight of the ingredients in the recipe amounts to 1.8 kg (4 lb) you need to pre-heat 8 l (14 pt) of water. But if you are using the popular thermostatically-controlled mash-cum-boiler you will need about an extra 1.2 l (2 pt) to make up for the amount that runs through the perforated basket and lies between this and the walls of the boiler itself. This extra will not affect the total amount of wort because the amount required is adjusted at a later stage.

Starch test   As already explained, during mashing starch is converted to fermentable sugars; this is of course the whole idea of the mashing period. It is therefore helpful to know when all the starch has been converted to sugar. In the normal way when mashing at a temperature of 65°C (150°F), all conversion to sugars should be completed within an hour. So after an hour you put a little of the liquid, free of grains, onto a plate, preferably a white one so that colour change is quickly noticed. Using a dropper, add a drop or two of tincture of iodine to this small sample. If the sample turns blue or blue-black, starches are still present and all conversion to sugars is not yet complete. Mashing should therefore be continued until there is no change of colour in the sample when a second or third test is made. Discard the sample and use a fresh plate for each test.

Even when the test shows that all starch has been converted, mashing must be continued for up to four hours or longer if you want to leave it to look after itself. After the starch has been converted and mashing continued for hours, the heat may be switched off, the boiler wrapped in a blanket and the mash left until you are ready to sparge, but in any case not longer than eight hours. The temperature will fall very slowly during this time, but this does not matter provided all starches are converted before the temperature begins to fall. Generally three hours at 65°C (150°F) is quite suitable, though many operators have their own special times, and then the temperature may be allowed to fall slowly until you are ready for sparging.

Balancing the acid content of the mash   This is an extremely complex business for which beginner brewers are not likely to be prepared. It is also difficult to explain without becoming far too technical, and it is unlikely that beginners would want to become involved in the sort of chemical analysis that is required. First it is important to obtain from your local water board a breakdown of the chemical content of your water supply. And this, when you get it, will complicate matters even more unless you are a chemist – and if you are you will not be reading this book. But the fact remains that salts in the water in your district and the weak organic acids in brewing ingredients play their part in the overall effect. Adding acids like those added to wines is not always effective because of what are known as buffering agents – agents that lessen or prevent their effect altogether; lessening the acid content of a mash is also far more complicated than in wine-making.

Therefore, although the acid content of the mash is important from the enzyme reaction point of view, a simpler middle course may be followed. This is not quite so effective or reliable as correcting what is known as the pH value, but it is the best the beginner can achieve without taking a course in the chemistry of water analysis.

This simple middle course is to decide whether or not the water in your district is soft or hard. And this is easily done by looking in your kettle. If it is furred up the water is hard, if it is not, then the water is soft. Furthermore, soft water will always produce a better lather on your chin if, like me, you use shaving soap. The water in my district therefore is soft.

Pale, bitter and similar types of beers are best made with hard water, while stouts, brown ales, mild beers and some lagers are best made with soft water. One level teaspoonful of gypsum, or what is known as water treatment salts, may be stirred into every 5 l (1 gall) of water to harden it before use. On the other hand boiling hard water will soften it, but the water must be allowed to cool and any precipitate left behind when the water is used. Since all this tends to complicate rather than simplify matters it is often best for beginners to start by making the kind of beer their water is best suited for.

Sparging

The whole idea in sparging is to wash the spent grains free of fermentable sugar adhering to them. There is usually quite a lot and as this is an important part of the wort we must wash off as much as possible into the wort as it is drained from the grains.

Stodgy mashes should be thinned a little by adding a small amount of hot water at a temperature of not over 65°C (150°F). This should be done sometime during the mashing process, but not before the starch test shows that all starches have been converted to sugar and at least an hour before sparging is begun.

The sparge water should be prepared before drawing off the wort from the

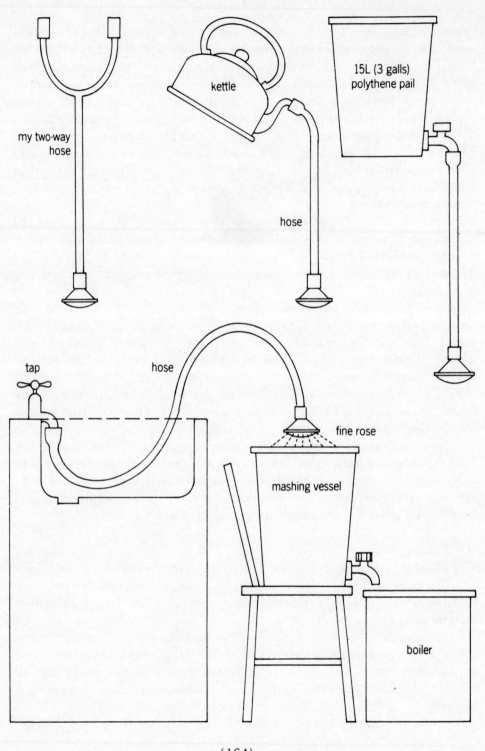

my two-way
hose

kettle

15L (3 galls)
polythene pail

hose

hose

tap

hose

fine rose

mashing vessel

boiler

(164)

grains and it is well to prepare 5 l (1 gall) for roughly a 10 l (2 gall) batch of beer. Since the sugar will wash off better if the water is hot it should be heated to about 75°C (170°F) but not above 82°C (180°F). If your mashing vessel is deep (as is the case with the Burco boiler) pouring the sparge water from a jug or kettle will prove awkward as you will not be able to direct the flow where it is needed. But if you are using a bag to contain the wort (as when an ordinary thermostatically-controlled heater is used with an ordinary fermentation pail) a jug or kettle will do quite well, provided you pour very carefully and gently, directing the water into the middle of the mash and gradually in circles moving towards the edge. This operation should be started after you have begun to run the wort from the grains. Open the trap slowly, allowing the wort to run in little more than a trickle, and collect the first two or three pints, in a suitable vessel. This will be very murky and can be returned to the grains so that they filter out much of the murkiness. But do not do this until the top of the bed of grains appears above the wort. When the top of the bed is free of wort (let me describe this as watching water disappear through shingle) the murky wort can be poured very carefully over the grains. Sparging can then commence and this should be so slow that at no time does the water you are using rise above the grains. Open the tap wider so that the wort runs out as fast as you sparge. The grains should not be stirred or disturbed during sparging because while you are washing off the sugar the grain-husks act as a filter to hold back matter that might otherwise create a clearing problem if it was washed through.

After some sparging, take a few husks into your hand. If they are very sticky, more sparging should be carried out. However do not use so much sparge water that you produce more wort than the amount of beer you are proposing to make. For example if you are making 10 l (2 gall) of beer do not produce more than 10 l (2 gall) of wort. However, this last sentence must be qualified. During boiling (see p. 166) some loss will occur, so you can, if necessary, sparge to

Sparging

With the recipes here you may use about 12½ l (2½ galls) of water for sparging. This, together with the amount of water used at the outset, will produce roughly 22½ l (4½ galls) of wort. Some loss will occur during boiling so the extra wort at this stage will be lost.

How you, personally, go about your sparging will depend on resources or whim. Either a kettle replenished from the hot water tap or a pail with a tap may be used, but they must have a spray attachment as shown here. The water must be hot to wash off the sticky sugar adhering to the grain's husks.

My own arrangement is quite simple. I ensure that the water is running at about 71-76°C (160-170°F) – that is, hot to the back of the hand but not too hot to bear. My two-way hose from a washing machine no longer in use enables me to run both hot and cold water simultaneously if necessary.

produce 1.2 l (2 pt) extra for each 10 l (2 gall) of beer you are making. All this is general purpose instruction which you will vary to suit yourself as your experience grows, but it is as well to observe certain limits to start with.

Boiling and Cooling

As already mentioned, boiling is essential in brewing not only to sterilize the wort and so destroy the causes of spoilage which in beer-making are more or less the same as in wine-making, but also to 'fix' the quality of the beer. This 'fixing' is brought about by the high temperature which destroys the enzymes which have brought about the desirable changes in the grains, that is the conversion to sugars of the starches present. These enzymes, if not destroyed, would carry on too long. Boiling also tends to coagulate waste matter that could cause clouding of the beer at a later stage. And of course boiling serves to extract the flavour from the hops and generally stabilize the beer.

The hops are added loose either just before boiling or immediately sparging is complete. Either way the hops remain in the wort during the whole of the boiling process. If you use compressed hops, do make sure that they are well-broken up before adding them. Always weigh your hops to the exact amount given in the recipe.

During the early stages of boiling, the wort often spits or kicks and thumps, and this can lead to some loss of wort if the vessel is too full. Adding water to make good the loss would not be good practice because you would be adding water containing none of the sugars that have spilled onto the floor. So it is important to allow for the boiling-up of the wort by using a vessel large enough to contain the wort while leaving about a quarter of the vessel empty as headroom. This of course means not making a larger amount of beer than your vessel can conveniently accommodate. However boiling about 20 l (4 gall) in a 25 l (5 gall) boiler should present no problem. You could, if making a 20 l (4 gall) lot, sparge the wort to produce say 17½ l (3½ gall), then boil this and when the boiling is complete stir in a further 2½ l (4 pt) of boiling water.

Normally boiling is for one to one and a half hours, but it is wise after one hour to take a small sample of the wort into a clear glass or Pyrex jug. As the sample cools, small lumps of protein waste-matter about the size of a letter 'o' in the print of this book, though not so regular in shape, will be seen either in suspension or settled on the bottom. Tilt the jug and hold it to the light so that these become clearly visible in the still hazy wort. When this stage is reached – and it might be necessary to make three or four tests after one hour's boiling – you can consider that the wort has been boiled enough and the heat may be switched off.

Five minutes or so after the heat is switched off the beer in the boiler will appear quite dark or even black and quite clear. Any floating debris including

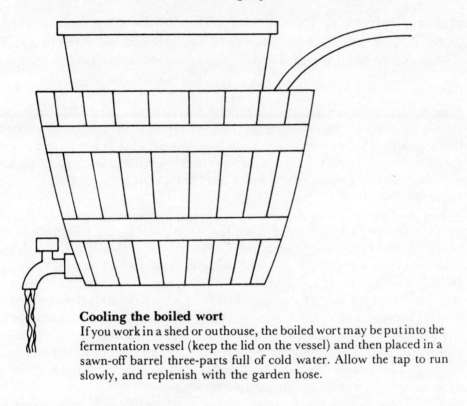

Cooling the boiled wort
If you work in a shed or outhouse, the boiled wort may be put into the
fermentation vessel (keep the lid on the vessel) and then placed in a
sawn-off barrel three-parts full of cold water. Allow the tap to run
slowly, and replenish with the garden hose.

hops seeds can be skimmed off. Almost immediately after the heat is switched
off the hops, along with the protein matter you saw in the jug, will settle to the
bottom of the boiler. The hops form a filter bed through which the wort is
drawn off into the fermenting vessel. When all the wort is drawn off about 1.2 l
(2 pt) of hot water may be poured very gently onto the bed of hops to wash
through any sugary wort they may be holding back. Normally the wort is left to
cool and the hops to form their bed for about fifteen minutes before the wort is
drawn off. Thereafter cooling must be as rapid as possible. Commercial brewers use refrigeration plant, but the best we can do is to stand the fermenting
vessel in a tub of cold water. If this tub or sawn-off barrel is fitted with a tap the
water as it warms can be run off and more cold water added. If you work in an
outhouse or shed, the tub can be filled and the tap opened so that the water
drips out, while a garden hose can keep the tub full of cold water. How long
cooling takes depends on whether you are working indoors or in a shed, and on
the ambient temperature. In winter cooling will be much faster than in summer. Rapid cooling prevents the causes of spoilage getting a hold before the
yeast we have ready to add, or 'pitch' in, can start the wort fermenting and so
form its own protective cloud of gas above the wort. So do think up some means

of cooling the wort quickly to 15-18°C (60-65°F). When this temperature is reached, or when the wort is luke-warm, the yeast may be stirred in.

The yeast is best made into a starter as described on p. 170.

Fermentation

In wine-making fermentation is the process that turns our musts into wines and so in beer-making fermentation is the process that turns our worts into foaming beers. However before fermentation the hydrometer must be used to ascertain the specific gravity and this must be adjusted to give the amount of alcohol required. And I must repeat: DO NOT BE TEMPTED TO MAKE YOUR BEERS OVERSTRONG.

You may need to adjust the wort. If, for example, the recipe used is designed to make 20 l (4 gall) of beer, the amount in the fermenting vessel must be brought up to this amount with boiled water that has cooled. The hydrometer reading is then taken, sugar added if necessary (as described on p. 57) and the yeast then stirred in. If you are using a thermostatically-controlled fermentation vessel keep the wort at a temperature of 15-17°C (60-63°F). If the temperature is lower than 15°C (60°F) fermentation can become too slow; above 17°C (63°F) it can become too rapid. A good steady ferment, neither too fast nor too slow, ensures quality in the finished product. It is of the utmost importance that the fermenting beer be covered closely either with a lid if your vessel has one or with unpunctured sheet polythene tied down tightly.

As in wine-making, as fermentation proceeds, more and more yeast is produced. Whereas in wine-making we see the fruit particles or skins and pips on the surface pushed up by the upsurge of gas, in brewing we see an ever-increasing growth of yeast on the surface of the brew. At some stage, usually between six and ten hours after adding the yeast, a thick head will be seen on the surface and this will be flecked with thrown-up residues, debris and other matter that is not required in the beer. If this is left, it can eventually settle into the beer and spoil it. So skim off the top of the head and the thrown-up waste matter, but leave a layer of cleaner-looking yeast underneath. And do remember to wipe off any scum left adhering to the inside of the fermentation vessel after skimming with a scalded cloth.

When a second thick head has formed, the top, which will be dirty but not quite so dirty as the first, should be skimmed lightly to leave the main head nice and clean underneath.

If your yeast seems slow to form a head it may need rousing. My grandfather and my father used something which looked like a small two-rung ladder with a pole running through the middle, so that it resembled two small ladders joined to the middle pole. However the best we can use today is a wooden spoon to give a good stirring. As fermentation slows down (this will be shown by less and less yeast formation, or you can use the hydrometer if you wish), the yeast should be skimmed off and the beer put into 5 or 10 l (1 or 2 gall) jars and fermentation locks fitted. If you use the hydrometer to decide how fermentation is progressing it would be wise to put the beer under fermentation locks at a reading of 1015. Putting the beer under locks is important because the width of the top of the fermentation vessel and the small amount of gas being produced would together expose the beer to the same causes of spoilage as are encountered in wine-making. Under fermentation locks the beer is perfectly safe.

Jars may not be very suitable if large amounts of beer are being brewed and in this case what are known as 'wine fives' may be used. These are polythene containers obtainable from off-licences where they are used for wine. Normally they hold 25 l (5 gall). Before use they must be washed free of all traces of wine and then sterilized with sulphite solution as used in wine-making. If such a receptacle is used, the tap may be removed and a fermentation lock and bung fitted into the hole. The vessel will of course have to be turned so that the fermentation lock is uppermost. These containers reach off-licences in strong cardboard support containers because the vessels themselves are not very strong. Use the support containers for added strength.

When fermentation has ceased you have the choice of priming and bottling or using a pressure barrel (see p. 157).

Yeast and Yeast Starter

If you can obtain yeast from a brewery than by all means use it. Usually it has the consistency of icecream. Only about half an ounce is needed for your starter bottle for, say, a 25 l (5 gall) brew. Dried brewer's yeast in powder granules or tablet form is common and popular. All are quite suitable. Most of these are known as top-fermenting yeasts, but the bottom-fermenting yeasts are also suitable. There is a good deal of difference in the types and their reaction in the wort, though both produce the alcohol required in roughly the same time. Whereas the top fermenting kind builds up a yeast head on the surface of the wort and builds it up again after skimming, the bottom-fermenting kind usually falls to the bottom of the vessel shortly after the first skim, one skim usually being enough for this kind. Whichever you choose it is always wise, as in wine-making, to get the wort into a state of vigorous fermentation as soon as possible after the temperature has been brought down to 15°C (60°F), to create that all-important cloud of carbon dioxide gas above the wort which protects it against contamination by bacteria. The wort, if not fermenting in a very short while, can become affected quite readily. So do not hesitate to make a nucleus ferment of your beer yeast between three to six hours before it will be needed. Some yeasts start fermenting in an hour while others need longer to get going. Your experience later on will tell you when to start your necleus with whichever yeast you are using.

Making a nucleus   'Nucleus' is a somewhat technical term; in this case it just means a colony of active yeast (often called activated yeast) which we shall produce in our starter bottle.

All that is needed for the average-size brew is about 3 dl (½ pt) of water boiled in an enamel unchipped saucepan with a dessertspoonful of sugar and malt extract dissolved in it. When this has cooled to lukewarm (about 15°C (60°F)) it is poured into a narrow-necked bottle, using a funnel, and the yeast is then added. The neck of the bottle should be plugged with a firm knob of cotton wool or fitted with the teat of a baby-feed bottle pierced from the inside with a needle. This small hole will form an outlet for the excess carbon dioxide gas that builds up. If you use a wide-necked bottle you can fit a fermentation lock provided you have a suitable-sized cork bored to take one. But do not use larger than a pint-size bottle for such a small nucleus. If your starter bottle is of dark glass a fermentation lock with its sterilizing solution (see p. 28) will soon tell you when fermentation is nicely on the go. With a clear glass bottle you will be able to see for yourself. Keep the nucleus in the warm the whole time and when the time comes for 'pitching' the yeast into the wort, shake up the nucleus and pour all the yeast into the wort. And don't forget to cover as advised or to fit the lid to your fermenting vessel at once.

Guinness yeast   To obtain Guinness yeast buy a pint bottle of Guinness and let it stand in a really cold place (but not the fridge) for at least twelve hours before making it into a starter or nucleus. This yeast may need twenty-four hours to become active, so plan well in advance of requirements and remember that the yeast must be fully active before it is pitched – that is, it should not just have started to ferment.

When you are ready, pour off the Guinness very carefully leaving about 3.5 cm (1½ in) in the bottle. Boil about 3 dl (½ pt) of water and into this pour a teaspoonful of sugar and a dessertspoonful of malt. Stir until thoroughly dissolved and when cool pour into the Guinness bottle, shake well, plug the neck with cotton wool (or, as mentioned earlier, fit the teat of a baby-feed bottle) and leave in a warm place until the yeast is fully active. If you put your ear close to the top of the bottle after twenty-four hours you should be able to hear the gentle fizzing of fermentation. If you prefer to use a clear glass bottle you may do so, but make sure you obtain all the Guinness yeast deposit by twisting and shaking the Guinness bottle before pouring into the clear glass one.

Sugars

In wine-making we use a lot of sugar because, except when using concentrated grape juices, grapes or dried fruits, there is very little sugar in the initial must.

In beer-making we use very little ordinary sugar because we produce sugars from the malt during mashing. However, it is important with some beers to add certain sugars for varying effects and adding flavours to the finished product. But white granulated or ordinary household sugar should always be used for priming and for adjusting the gravity when this is necessary before fermentation is started off.

Invert sugar   This is usually purchased as a solid brown sticky mass tasting not unlike the sweetmeat fudge. It can also be purchased near-white, with a hint of pale gold about it. The coarse brown is used to give a 'nutty' flavour to beers where this is needed. It can be made in the home by boiling household sugar in water to which citric acid has been added, but this does not have the flavour of the brown sort.

Brown sugar   Demerara, soft brown, and what was once known as foot sugar (is this still available?) and Barbados have their uses, but be careful with them.

Glucose chips   These look like oversized road-surfacing chips but on the white side. Expensive, but you might like to try a small experiment with them.

Black (green) treacle and golden syrup   The most that should go into a brew is a tablespoonful of black treacle to not less than 10 l (2 gall). Golden syrup may be used to give a slightly 'nutty' flavour. It spoils the flavour of most wines so you may not like it in beers.

Darkening beers   Brown ales and stouts are very dark in colour. It is often necessary to darken them and at the same time produce in the finished product the extra flavour that it should have. Caramel satisfies these requirements quite admirably, but it must be used with care. To overdarken could spoil the flavour. A good way to go about this operation is to add the caramel in stages, taking a small sample of the near-boiling or boiling wort into a Pyrex jug after each addition until you have the colour just right. Before any colouring is added the wort should first be checked to see if colouring is necessary. Do remember that the overcolouring cannot be reversed.

Getting a Head

The head on a glass of beer is just as important to most drinkers as the beer underneath. I am one of those who regard headless beer as unappetizing.

On my first trip to Southern Ireland I was shown how the publican produces pints of Guinness from the barrel. Under the bar were about twenty pints of Guinness froth and in the bottom of each there was a varying amount of Guinness – half an inch to perhaps two inches. Gradually the publican added a little more until the first one could be put on the bar with a frothy head of cream. The process continued all evening so that when an Irishman called for his national diet he did not have to wait for it. And if you ever go to the Emerald

Isles, never try to keep up with the native when he's drinking steadily. I have seen my late father-in-law drink seventeen pints of the stuff and walk home as if he had been to a tea party. In France however the suggestion of a head on a glass of beer seems to offend the nicest instincts of the bartender, for the devil guillotines it immediately, most often with a lolly stick. The fact is that nowhere in France could I get a decent beer. There may be a lot wrong with old England right now, but at least we can still get a decent beer or make it for ourselves – and surely that counts for something.

On well-made beer the head should form naturally. This is brought about by the carbon dioxide gas in its effort to escape. But rising to the surface it brings with it minute invisible solids which help to form the head. If the bubbles are large they form a rough-broken head that breaks down quickly, but if they are small they help to make a creamy head. The longer the beer is stored in bottles (bottled beer that is) the better the gas is absorbed into the beer and so the bubbles when they rise are smaller. But to keep bottled beers too long would have the reverse effect. Three to five weeks after priming is usually about right, but the experience of the individual brewer will tell him after a time how long to keep a particular brew before using it, bearing in mind that head formation and retention are important.

Formation of a head on a glass of beer can be prevented by the slightest trace of greasiness on the glass. Indeed if a glass is not spotlessly clean and brightly polished a head, if it forms at all, will vanish quickly. Even drinkers with a greasy skin (like myself) will deposit from his lips a tiny amount of skin grease that may prevent a head forming on the second pint put into the same glass. Many years ago I explained this to a publican at a popular local when draught beer was practically the only beer drunk. It vexed him that my second pint never had a head on it. And he (how different from today when you have to take it or leave it) insisted on serving me with a fresh glass every time. One of the last of the real oldstyle landlords who considered his customers above all else!

Beer stored in gas-pressured barrels will form a good head, but much depends on the ingredients used in the brewing. Barley, flaked maize and wheat flour help to produce head-forming materials which are brought to the surface with the upsurge of escaping gas. But this is not to say that these adjuncts should be used in recipes that do not call for them because they have an effect upon the beer as well and this is not always required. It is often a matter of trial and error to find out precisely what you want by way of head-forming materials while taking into account their effects upon the flavour of the beers into which they are incorporated.

Heading liquids Heading liquids and powders are available and while these will put a head on your beer, and one that will stay there, they are not the answer to everybody's heading problem. Before using these it would be wise to see how you get on without them and to use them as a last resort. In any case I have found that the amounts recommended by most suppliers produce too much head. Furthermore if the recommended amount is put into a barrel and the natural heading process is satisfactory, when the beer is drawn from the pressure barrel you may find that you have the same trouble as the Irish landlord mentioned at the beginning of this section, although that chap did not have a pressure barrel; it was the good old-fashioned wooden sort with a tap. So make your beers and see how things go before turning to artificial aids that may not be as helpful as they are intended to be. If you do resort to them, try using half the amount recommended by the supplier (or even less). Otherwise you may find that you have all head and no beer. Oh, calamity!

Sterilizing

Sterilizing utensils is just as important in beer-making as in wine-making. It is pointless to put sterilized beer into bottles which may contain wild yeasts and bacteria, and all bottles, jars, funnels and so on must therefore be sterilized with the same solution as given for use in wine-making (see p. 39).

Boilers and other utensils which will be boiled during the brewing process need not be treated. The grist – barley grains and other materials prepared for mashing – need not be treated because the hot water with which they are mixed and the temperature at which the mash is kept will keep it safe until it is boiled after sparging. The boiling of the wort is for the purpose of destroying wild yeast and bacteria that may be present and at the same time 'fixing' the beer. This means that the boiling destroys the enzymes which were busy during the mashing process to prevent further action by them and so 'fix' the beer.

Screw stoppers – you are lucky if you have them – may be sterilized in the sulphite solution. New rings are obtainable from home wine supply shops for the stoppers of screw-top bottles if you need them. Crown caps lined with cork should be dipped in boiling water because it is unwise to allow metal to come into contact with the sulphite solution. Crown caps lined with polythene or nylon may be treated similarly. Don't forget to put sterilizing solution in the fermentation locks when using these. And remember to wash out pressure barrels thoroughly and to sterilize them with sulphite solution before putting beer into them.

20
GENERAL PROCEDURE: SUMMARY

From the foregoing pages it will be seen that the procedure is:

Choose your recipe.

Mix the malt grains (cracked if necessary) and any adjuncts (flakes, wheat flour etc) well together in their dry state. If using dried malt extracts or those in syrup form do not include in this operation.

Mix dry mixed materials carefully with preheated water.

Mash at temperatures given for times stated.

Do starch test. Repeat if necessary.

Draw off some of the wort – about a quart to each gallon of beer being made – and begin sparging.

Continue sparging and return drawn-off wort carefully to the mash.

Continue sparging to make wort up to roughly the amount of beer being made.

Bring wort to the boil and when nearly boiling stir in any malt extracts being used and add the hops.

Boil.

Cool as quickly as possible. Some loss will occur during boiling, so make up to the amount of beer you are making with boiled water that has cooled. This will help to bring the temperature down.

Check temperature occasionally and when cooled to 15°C (60°F) take your hydrometer reading and adjust the gravity as necessary.

Add 'pitch' and stir in active yeast.

Ferment and skim.

(174)

General Procedure: Summary

Check fermentation and when slowing down transfer to jars without letting too much yeast deposit get into the jars.

Fit fermentation lock and continue fermenting in a warm place.

When the beer is still and clear, when all fermentation has ceased, siphon the clear beer into a fermentation pail or similar receptacle, prime (add dissolved sugar) and then bottle or put into pressure barrels.

21

MAKING BEERS WITH READY-TO-USE INGREDIENTS

The many ready-prepared packs, canned worts and such like really are worth the consideration of beginner beer-makers. These are available from almost all wine supply shops, from some multiple chemists and from Boots who are becoming more interested in this supply business every day. They are simplicity itself to use, like most concentrated grape juices for wine-making, and while I have tried several, I cannot have tried them all.

One important point about these packs or prepared worts is that the manufacturers have prepared them to a certain formula and therefore they know how best to work with them. You must follow the directions supplied with them and these vary considerably with each manufacturer and type of wort, brown ale, bitter beer, light ale or as the case may be.

However I have found in many cases, and I have even had people complain to me about it as if it were my fault, that when following the suppliers directions some beer-makers finish up with an inch or more of yeast deposit in the bottles. They complain that as soon as they open the bottle the deposit rises to cloud the beer. This is caused of course by the gas contained in the beer; as soon as the bottle is opened it tries to escape and in so doing brings the yeast into suspension. This is a big problem and much depends on the amount of gas present. If there is a lot of gas pressure the yeast will rise as soon as the cork is taken off. If there is not too much, almost three-quarters of the beer can be poured before the yeast rises and there is usually enough to give the required sparkle (or fizziness, or gaseousness), but there is still some waste of beer. To avoid this, I suggest (contrary to my plea to follow the supplier's directions) that you deviate from the printed instructions just a little bit, in the following manner.

During fermentation, when there is a good head of yeast on the surface of the beer, it is wise to skim it off and wipe round the inside of the fermentation vessel with a scalded cloth to remove any yeast adhering to the sides just above the surface of the beer.

(176)

Most instructions with beer kits or canned worts advise fermenting for so many days and then bottling. The idea is to allow fermentation to go on inside the bottles and so charge the beer with gas. Now if fermentation is as good as the manufacturers anticipate, this direction is usually perfectly satisfactory. But, as all experienced wine and beer-makers will confirm, fermentation in the open fermentation vessel (covered of course) will vary in its vigour with each batch of wine or beer. Set instructions cannot apply to each fermentation, simply because no one can be sure in advance how much of the fermentable sugar in the wort will be used up during fermentation in the fermenting vessel and how much will remain to be used up when the beer is bottled. It follows then that you will not know whether fermentation will go on in bottle too long or not long enough. And since this fermentation in the bottle is what is producing that mass of yeast in each bottle and then causing it to rise just when it should not, a remedy must be found. The simple answer is to deviate from the method. Instead of bottling when advised in the written instructions, let the beer ferment until it stops. You can either leave it in the fermenting pail, safely covered of course, or put it into jars and fit fermentation locks. If you leave it in the pail you will see that the beer goes flat in appearance; it no longer froths and there are no bubbles breaking on the surface when you look closely across the

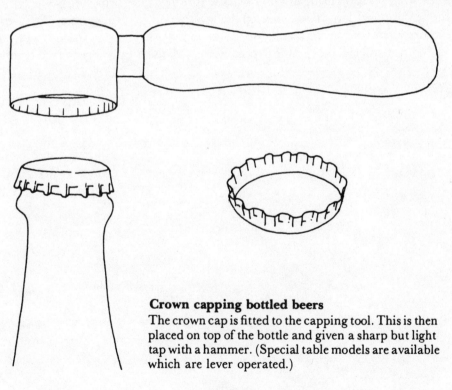

Crown capping bottled beers
The crown cap is fitted to the capping tool. This is then placed on top of the bottle and given a sharp but light tap with a hammer. (Special table models are available which are lever operated.)

(177)

surface of the beer (these bubbles look something like drizzle on a puddle). If you put the beer in jars under locks you will know when fermentation ceases by looking at the beer or the lock, or both.

When fermentation ceases the beer will be quite clear, but not brilliant. This is just as we want it, because it means that there is still a little yeast in suspension to carry on the ferment that we need.

So, bearing in mind that 65 g (2¼ oz) of sugar will give sufficient gas into 5 l (1 gall) of beer when it has been fermented out, the next operation is to ascertain the exact amount of beer you have and apportion the exact amount of sugar required for that amount. Put this in a saucepan, pour in a little of the beer and warm very gently, stirring constantly to dissolve the sugar. When all is dissolved, pour the sweetened sample into the fermenting vessel and siphon all the beer onto it to ensure thorough mixing. Then bottle and seal by whichever means you are employing – crown caps or screw stoppers. Keep the bottles in the warm for a week and then put in a cold place for a week or two. After this you should be able to pour the beer without the yeast rising, except that it is sure to move when the last drops of beer in the bottle begin to move.

One means of delaying this is to open the bottle slowly if you can and when you pour the beer, bring the glass up to the bottle. When the bottle is in the horizontal position bring another glass to it rather than bring the bottle back to the upright position. If you pour off the beer in one go, using as many glasses as required and without returning the bottle to the upright, you should, with care and a little experience, be able to pour almost all the beer before the yeast comes over.

22
MAKING BEERS WITH MALT EXTRACTS

When making beers with malt extracts you in effect start your beer-making halfway through the process. This is because the malts you use, whether dried or in syrup form, have been produced by a mashing process that we do not have to use. Only when using grain malt (see Chapter 23) do we need to put the ingredients (grain malts – malts still within the grain) through a mashing process to convert the starches to fermentable sugars. As the mashing process has been carried out for us, all we have to do is to carry on from where the manufacturers of the various malt extracts left off. So we have to dilute the malt extracts, add hops, boil up, allow to cool, add yeast and away we go. But it is important here to use the hydrometer to find the precise amount of fermentable sugars in the wort to enable us to control the alcohol content. We want beers as cool refreshing drinks and not soporific depressants. They should be low in alcohol compared with wines and generally 5% by volume is enough. You can make them lower or a little higher in alcohol if you wish, but I cannot see the point in this except where imitating a higher-than-average alcohol content commercial product.

As in wine-making 65 g (2¼ oz) of sugar will raise the reading by 5 on the hydrometer in 5 l (1 gall). If you want to raise it by 5 in 10 l (2 gall) you will need 130 g (4½ oz). And if you want to reduce the reading, when it is found to be a little too high, you merely add boiled water to reduce the sugar content.

Adjusting the gravity   There are special hydrometers for beer-making and thermometers too, and it is wise to use these. Hydrometer readings should always be taken when the wort is at the temperature of 15°C (60°F). This is standard. If the temperature is higher the wort is expanded by the warmth and you would get a lower reading than is actual fact. Similarly if the wort is cooler it is more compact or denser and you would get a higher reading than the correct figure. So always check the temperature before taking the hydrometer reading and

(179)

cool or warm the wort as necessary. Obviously it is best to check the temperature as the wort cools to avoid having to reheat the wort. Check and recheck
until it drops to 15°C (60°F). Having done this, take the hydrometer reading
and adjust if necessary as already explained. When to check temperature and
take the hydrometer reading is given in the method for malt extract beers on p.
184.

An important point to bear in mind when taking the hydrometer reading is
that beers, while they will ferment to dryness as wines do, will aways have a
reading of five or six on the hydrometer when all fermentation has ceased. To
allow for this it is wise to start off with a gravity five higher than you want. So if
you want the alcohol produced by a reading of 1040, you should start with a
reading of 1045. You will still get the alcohol required from the reading of 1040.

If you take a look at the table on p. 57 in the wine-making section you will
see how much alcohol this figure of 1040 will make. I have already explained
how to raise or lower the gravity according to the amount of alcohol you want to
make, so all you have to do is to start off with a gravity showing five higher on
the hydrometer than the alcohol content you want. And do bear in mind that
5% by volume is the absolute maximum for beers and that 4% makes them far
more refreshing and enjoyable.

Hops   It is best to use flavour-sealed whole hops, but these are not always
readily available. Dried, pressed hops give excellent results provided they are
not stale. Buy from a busy shop where stocks move quickly. The type or variety
of hops to use is very often a matter of choice and will in any case depend on the
type of beer you are making. Those suggested in the recipes are those I have
found to give good results, but you can use others if you wish.

Recipes Using Malt Extract

The recipes are designed to make 10 l (2 gall) of beer. This is the amount most
beginners like to make in order to get the feel of things and without going to too
much expense in case they do not like their first couple of tries. When they have
found the recipe that makes the beer they really like they can embark on making
25 or 50 l (5 or 10 gall) batches with confidence. The recipes are basic recipes.
That is to say they are for you to try first and alter later as you wish from time to
time, bearing in mind that different malts make for slightly different results and
that hops add tang, flavour and some preservative properties as well as some
natural acids which are desirable in any beer. By giving a basic recipe for, say,
brown ale or bitter you know the sort of beer to expect. But it does not follow
that it will be like your favourite commercial brown or bitter, because every
beer is different. There are so many brown ales, bitters, light ales and so on
turned out by the many different brewery groups, and each is almost com-

pletely different from the next. To give half a dozen recipes for light ales, brown ales or bitters would be no help at all; it would only confuse.

Everybody is evolving new recipes for making the same sort of beer so that eventually we may end up (as we can say has happened in wine-making with elderberries and some other fruits) with 20,000 ways of making brown ale, light ale or what have you. This sort of thing is no help to anybody, least of all to the beginner trying to decide what sort of beer to make a start with.

The method for all these recipes is on p. 184.

MILD BEER

900 g (2 lb) pale dried malt extract; 450 g (1 lb) dark malt extract; 40 g (1½ oz) hops (Fuggles preferred); top-fermenting beer yeast; water as in method

BITTER

1.125 kg (2½ lb) pale dried malt extract; 225 g (½ lb) dark malt extract; 40 g (1½ oz) hops (Goldings preferred); top-fermenting beer yeast; water as in method

PALE ALE
(Light Ale)

1.225 kg (2¾ lb) pale dried malt extract; 100 g (¼ lb) medium-dark dried malt extract; 40 g (1½ oz) hops (Goldings preferred); top-fermenting beer yeast; water as in method

BROWN ALE

900 g (2 lb) pale dried malt extract; 225 g (½ lb) medium-dark dried malt extract; 225 g (½ lb) dark dried malt extract; 40 g (1½ oz) hops (Northern Brewer preferred); lactose to taste (if sweetening is required); top-fermenting beer yeast; water as in method

LAGER TYPE

1.125 kg (2½ lb) DMS malt extract; 450 g (1 lb) pale dried malt extract; 40 g (1½ oz) hops (Saaz preferred); top-fermenting beer yeast; water as in method

STOUT

900 g (2 lb) pale malt extract; 450 g (1 lb) dark malt extract; 40 g (1½ oz) hops (Fuggles preferred); lactose to taste (if sweetening is required); water as in method

PORTER TYPE

450 g (1 lb) pale malt extract; 450 g (1 lb) dark malt extract; 450 g (1 lb) soft brown sugar; 40 g (1½ oz) hops (Fuggles preferred); water as in method

BARLEY WINE

Because we are using brewing ingredients this recipe for barley wine must come under the heading of brewing. Making barley wines from grain barley is a tiresome and quite complicated job, and since some very excellent barley wines can be made with malt extracts it is a good idea to use them. For anybody using grain barley to say that good barley wine cannot be made from malt extracts is like a wine-maker saying that good wines cannot be made from concentrated grape juices – when everybody knows that they can. I have tasted some quite excellent barley wine made from ready-prepared barley wine wort bought by the can; one was known as Edme concentrated barley wine wort. But this is another matter, and if you use a prepared wort you will have to follow the directions of the supplier.

Barley wine is usually in the region of 10-11% of alcohol by volume which means that it may be drunk in slightly larger quantities than the higher alcohol sorts. The recipe here makes for a wine of around 10-1.1% by volume, but by using more sugar as shown under the recipe you can make it the same strength as ordinary full-strength wines.

Barley wine is a sparkling wine and to obtain the effervescence it will have to be primed as for beers and bottled in small bottles fitted with crown caps or primed and then put into a small pressure barrel. Otherwise you can make it as an ordinary wine and then put·small amounts as required into a Sparklets siphon. If you do not like sparkling wines – and not everybody does – you can make it as an ordinary wine and use it as such. It is a matter of making it as you want it and not as other people say you should. After all, I cannot imagine entering a bar with someone and then having them turn round and tell me what I have got to drink.

1.350 kg (3 lb) Edme Super flavex; 225 g (½ lb) pale malt extract; 450 g (1 lb) granulated sugar; 225 g (½ lb) soft brown sugar; 25 g (1 oz) Goldings or Northern Brewer hops; good wine yeast

Wine yeast is needed because brewer's yeasts do not withstand alcohol as well as wine yeast, and may therefore stop fermenting before they should. To make a barley wine of the same strength as other wines use 225 g (½ lb) more pale malt and 225 g (½ lb) more soft brown sugar.

Follow the method for beers from malt extracts on p. 184, but ferment for ten days in the fermenting pail and then transfer to two 5 l (1 gall) jars, fit locks as

(183)

for wines and treat thereafter as wines. When fermentation has ceased, you can use as ordinary wine or prime as already mentioned and then treat as beer.

METHOD FOR ALL MALT EXTRACT BEERS AND BARLEY WINE

Ideally a 15 l (3 gall) boiler is required. If your boiler will not hold 10 l (2 gall) and at the same time leave one-third of the total capacity clear at the top, use the largest vessel you have as there must be plenty of room for boiling up. The rest of the water can be added later.

Put about 2.5 l (4 pt) of hot water in your vessel and add the malts, stirring until thoroughly dissolved. Add as much water as your vessel will hold (to leave one-third unfilled, but in any case not more than 10 l (2 gall)), and bring the mixture to the boil. When just about to boil stir in the hops. Then boil for one hour to extract all flavour from the hops.

The next step is either to strain out the hops through three or four thicknesses of muslin or, if your boiler is fitted with a tap, to run off the wort, stirring to keep the hops from blocking the outlet. Strain or run the wort into the fermenting pail and make up to 6.2 l (2¼ gall) with boiling water. This should leave you with 5 l (2 gall) of beer when fermentation is complete and the beer is taken off the initial deposit.

To speed cooling stand the vessel in a sink or other suitable vessel filled with cold water. Check temperature after the first half hour if vessel is standing in cold water or after one and a half hours if no cooling aid is provided. When the temperature reaches 15°C (60°F) take the hydrometer reading and adjust the gravity if necessary to the reading you require (as explained on p. 180), not forgetting to apportion sugar for the extra quart. Now add the starter bottle of yeast. Cover the vessel as for wine-making or fit the lid and ferment in the warm for three or four days. Skim the first heavy head of yeast off and discard it. With a scalded cloth wipe off any yeast adhering to the sides of the vessel and cover again at once.

The next step is to siphon the beer into 5 l (1 gall) jars of the sort used for wine-making and fit fermentation locks. Any beer that will not go into the jars may be put into a container such as a quart bottle. Plug the neck with a hard knob of cotton wool, or, better, with a fermentation lock if you have a cork of suitable size or the teat of a baby-feed bottle pierced from inside with a needle.

When fermentation has ceased and the beer is clear you have two alternatives: to bottle or to put it into pressure barrels. Either way some priming is necessary to condition the beer and to create sparkle and head-forming carbon dioxide gas. Pressure barrels fitted with CO_2 cylinders (as used in all bars these days, but on more elaborate lines) are shown on p. 158. Beer-capping is shown on p. 177.

Priming Siphon the clear beer into a fermentation vessel and ascertain how much you have. For each 5 l (1 gall) put 65 g (2¼ oz) of white sugar (not more) into an enamel saucepan with a little of the beer. Warm gently, stirring to dissolve the sugar, and when all is dissolved, stir into the bulk and then bottle your beer.

I prefer this method of adding the priming sugar, rather than adding a level teaspoonful of dry sugar to each bottle as many people advocate, because you are assured that the sugar is dissolved properly.

Note

In the case of brown ales or stout that need sweetening stir in a dessertspoonful of lactose to every 5 l (1 gall) before adding the priming sugar or putting the beer into a pressure barrel. Taste for sweetness, using a little more if necessary.

Bottled beers should be kept in the warm for about a week and then moved to a cool place for a week or perhaps two before using, depending on how long you can wait before sampling.

After priming some fermentation will go on inside the bottles or pressure barrel and it is wise to allow two weeks in a warm atmosphere and a week in a cool place before using the beer.

23
MAKING BEERS WITH GRAIN MALTS

As mentioned earlier, making beers using grain malts (that is, malts still within the grain) is a little more complicated than using malt extracts because of the need for what we call mashing. However the different processes are explained under their own headings in Chapter 19 and I do hope that all is clear.

You will not find an abundance of recipes for the very simple reason that to have a dozen for bitter or stout or brown ale would confuse you rather than help. Far better to give one basic recipe for each to enable you to assess whether you are going to like it as it is – and you may have to acquire a taste for it – or whether you want to try the same recipe next time with a slightly varied amount of ingredients. As I have gone to some trouble to explain, in wine- and beer-making it is a matter of personal choice. I do not like the light ales turned out by certain commercial brewers, nor do I like the bitters made by other brewers. And so it will be with the recipes here. You may like the results first time, but you may not. You may remark, 'not bad at all, but not quite what I am after.' And then you put on your thinking cap and ask yourself what is lacking, whether there is too much of 'this' and not enough of 'that'. You will find yourself experimenting to find exactly what you want. And I am sure you will find it very quickly.

Preparing the Grains

It is always best to buy cracked grains as to mill or crack them yourself usually results in either crushing, if you are not careful, or under-cracking, if you are too cautious. And since with pale malts the right degree of cracking is essential it is best to obtain the cracked variety.

Roasted malts, crystal malts and black malts are usually obtained whole and the cracking has to be done at home. But as the degree of cracking is not as important with these as it is with the pale sorts, a rolling-pin or even a beer bottle will do. Just run it over the grains with gentle pressure so that the inside of the grains is exposed and can therefore be subjected to enzyme action.

Mixing various grains should be done in the dry state; the hands should be plunged into the grains raised up and the grains allowed to fall through the fingers to ensure thorough mixing. Any adjuncts such as flaked maize may be mixed in at the same time.

When thoroughly mixed the lot is put into the mashing vessel. The hot brewery liquor (water), with the water treatment salts or gypsum already added if either is necessary, is then mixed well with the grains. Remember that the water should be in the region of 75°C (170°F), but not hotter. The water should be allowed to run in fairly slowly while the grains are being stirred to ensure even distribution of the water and its heat. If you are using the Burco boiler with the lift-out basket, you can first bring the water up to about 82°C (180°F), run it into another container, insert the basket into the the boiler, then ladle the water and the grains in at the same time. The heated water may be a little too hot or it may have cooled a little more than it should in being transferred to the second vessel, so do check the temperature because at this stage it is most important.

24
RECIPES

The recipes here are designed to make 20 l (4 gall) of beer. Whether you make this amount or not is entirely your own affair, and much will depend on the size of utensils available. If you want to make 10 l (2 gall) lots to start with merely halve all ingredients given in the recipe. But do not change the mashing times or boiling times. These must remain as they are. Whether you make 10 litres or 100, 2 gallons or 50 at a time the processes still require the same amount of time.

As already explained, these are basic recipes, one for each type of popular beer. It would be no use at all giving half a dozen recipes for each because you would not know which one to choose. Giving you one basic recipe for each type gives you the chance to find out whether that beer is what you want or whether you need to alter the recipes slightly before using it again.

Bear in mind that hops add bitterness, some tang or bite, a little flavour and some preservative properties. Malt makes for fullness, flavour and body. Pale malts are used mainly for the beer itself. The darker roasted and other types are used for special effects, as are certain sugars and adjuncts such as flaked maize, flaked rice and wheat flour.

For all recipes follow the general procedure on p. 174.

STOUT

To make 20 litres (4 gallons).

2.250 kg (5 lb) pale malt (crushed); 225 g (8 oz) roasted barley (crack it yourself); 100 g (4 oz) black malt (crack it yourself); 2 dessertspoonsful black (green) treacle; 40 g (1½ oz) hops (Northern Brewer); top-fermenting yeast; 225-275 g (8-10 oz) lactose for sweetening

Follow the general procedure. Mash at 65°C (150°F) minus or plus the odd degree for 3 hours. At this stage the mash tun may be wrapped in a blanket and left overnight. If you do this regulate the thermostat to 60°C (140°F) for 1 hour and then switch off the power supply. Sparge first thing in the morning.

The lactose must be thoroughly mixed with 6 dl (1 pt) of the wort and stirred in before boiling. The treacle should also be stirred in before boiling and adding the hops.

BROWN ALE

To make 20 litres (4 gallons).

1.8 kg (4 lb) pale malt (crushed); 150 g (6 oz) black malt (crack it yourself); 150 g (6 oz) flaked maize; 150 g (6 oz) roasted malt (crack it yourself); 450 g (1 lb) soft brown sugar or brown invert sugar; 50 g (2 oz) hops (Fuggles or Northern Brewer); 275 g (10 oz) lactose for sweetening; top-fermenting yeast.

Follow the general procedure. Mash at 64.5-66.5°C (148-150°F) for 3 hours or overnight (see note under recipe for stout), then sparge. The soft brown sugar should be thoroughly stirred into the near-boiling wort just before the hops are added. Do this slowly so that there is no risk of the sugar sinking to burn on the bottom of the boiler.

The lactose should be thoroughly mixed with 6 dl (1 pt) or so of hot wort in a separate vessel and then stirred in.

BITTER

Hard water is best. To make 20 litres (4 gallons).

2.250 kg (5 lb) pale malt (crushed); 450 g (1 lb) glucose chips; 125 g (5 oz)

crystal malt (crack it yourself); 100 g (4 oz) flaked rice; 75 g (3 oz) hops (Goldings); 75 g (3 oz) demerara sugar; top-fermenting yeast

Follow general procedure. Mash at 65-66°C (149-151°F) for 3 hours or over-night (see note under recipe for stout), then sparge. The demerara sugar and glucose chips must be dissolved in hot wort in a separate container and stirred in just before the hops are added. After that the lot is brought to the boil. Boil for 1½-2 hours.

MILD ALE

The popular draught mild beer. Soft water is best. To make 20 litres (4 gallons).

1.8 kg (4 lb) pale malt (crushed); 150 g (6 oz) crystal malt (crack it yourself); 150 g (6 oz) black malt (crack it yourself); 450 g (1 lb) demerara or soft brown sugar; 50 g (2 oz) hops (Northern Brewer or Fuggles); top-fermenting yeast

May need darkening (see notes under brown ale recipe). Follow general procedure. Mash at 64.5-65.5°C (148-150°F) for 3½ hours. Allow to cool to 55°C (130°F). Then sparge. The sugar should be gently and slowly added to the near-boiling wort just before the hops are added, making sure that it is stirred in well the whole time it is being added.

LIGHT ALE

To make 20 litres (4 gallons).

2 kg (4½ lb) pale malt (crushed); 75 g (3 oz) crystal malt (crack it yourself); 450 g (1 lb) household (white granulated) sugar; 65 g (2½ oz) hops (Goldings); top-fermenting yeast

Follow general procedure. Mash at 65-66°C (149-151°F) for 2½ -3 hours, then sparge. Just before the wort is boiling, stir in the sugar slowly, stirring all the time it is being added to ensure that it is thoroughly dissolved.

Boil for 1½ hours.

PALE ALE

Draught pale ale type. To make 20 litres (4 gallons).

2.250 kg (5 lb) pale malt (crushed); 450 g (1 lb) soft brown sugar; 225 g (½ lb) crystal malt (crack it yourself); 100 g (4 oz) flaked rice; 65 g (2½ oz) hops (Kent Goldings); top-fermenting yeast

Follow general procedure. Mash at 65-66°C (149-151°F) for 3 hours, then sparge. Just before the wort is boiling, pour in the sugar slowly, stirring the whole time to ensure that all the sugar is dissolved.

Boil for 1½-2 hours.

LIFFEY WATER

Or 'The Little People's Stout'. To make 20 litres (4 gallons).

If only we could make Guinness as they do in Dublin and London. Many years ago I visited the Dublin breweries and watched in awe as the Guinness went out by the tanker load. Despite my vigilance I saw nothing in the brewery to give a hint as to how they get that extra something into their Guinness. This used to be my favourite drink and in my view there is nothing to compare with it. It has everything. Bitterness, sweetness, dryness without being dry, roughness, smoothness, a lot of tang, a lot of colour and a creamy head that clings until the last dregs have been swallowed with relish. Alas, I am no longer allowed to drink it!

Making a top-class imitation of this beer is difficult and doubtless my recipe here will be improved upon. So go ahead you brewers with imagination and an experimental turn of mind, for doubtless you will make a better Guinness in a year or two's time.

Soft water is best for this.

2.250 kg (5 lb) pale malt (crushed); 150 g (6 oz) black malt (crack it yourself); 300 g (12 oz) roasted barley (crack it yourself); 2 tablespoonsful Barbados sugar; 50 g (2 oz) hops (Bullion); Guinness yeast (see p. 170)

Follow general procedure. Stir in the sugar just before the wort boils. Mash at 64.5-65.5°C (148-150°F) for 3 hours, or overnight if you wish allowing the temperature to fall to 57°C (135°F) but not below.

Bottled it should be kept for one month at least. In pressure barrels it should be left for at least two weeks. Be careful with the pressure otherwise you may get too much frothing and too little beer. Try this first in an ordinary polythene barrel without pressure. The priming sugar should have produced all the condition needed. If you use heading liquid use only half a teaspoonful to the 20 l (4 gall). Use less than this if you bottle this beer.

If you use a barrel without a pressure cylinder to start with, fit the cylinder after drawing off the first two pints.

LAGER

Hard water is best. To make 20 litres (4 gallons).

1.125 kg (2½ lb) pale malt (crushed); 900 g (2 lb) lager malt (crack it yourself, but only just enough to open the grains); 225 g (½ lb) glucose chips; 65 g (2½ oz) Saaz; lager yeast

Follow the general procedure. Mash at 65.5°C (150 °F) for 1½ hours and then at 60°C (140°F) for 4 hours.

Sparge in the usual way and before boiling dissolve the glucose chips in some of the hot wort. Boil for 1½ hours, then cool rapidly. Make up to 20 l (4 gall), check temperature and 'pitch' active lager yeast when temperature is 12-15°C (55-60°F). Ferment at this temperature throughout the fermentation period. Transfer to jars and fit locks after ten days and continue to ferment until fermentation ceases. Then prime and bottle. Or, if you prefer draught lager, prime and put into a pressure barrel. Keep for six weeks at least before use and on no account use a heading liquid or powder. After two weeks in a warm place to help the yeast ferment the priming sugar move to a cool place for one month.

Part III
IN CONCLUSION

25

A SPECIAL WORD TO MY READERS IN AMERICA AND CANADA

Because my books sell in enormous numbers in your countries it is right that I should have a special word for you all.

It will be seen that my wine recipes are for 5 l (1 gall) lots and that the beer recipes are for 10 and 20 l (2 and 4 gall) lots. Most beginners in England like to get the feel of things with these small amounts. But because you think so big in everything – possibly owing to the fact that your countries are so vast in size – you might not bother with such pifflingly small amounts. I understand that you think more on the lines of thirty to forty gallons at a time and I often wonder what you do with it all.

So just let me show you here how to adapt my recipes for your larger amounts. If making a 25 l (5 gall) batch of wine using my 5 l (1 gall) recipe, use four times the the amounts of all ingredients given and use 5 *American* gallons of water. If making 50 l (10 gall) use eight times the amounts of all ingredients given and use 10 *American* gallons of water.

When making beers using the 10 or 20 l (2 or 4 gall) recipes exactly the same principle applies. All this is necessary because the American gallon is different from ours. In your countries, as here, there are a great many home wine- and beer-making shops ready to serve your every need and I understand that most of them do a brisk trade in mail order. A list of suppliers in your countries appears at the end of this book. You will find that there are very many different sorts of concentrated grape juices available, as well as many concentrated fruit juices and pulps known in your countries as wine or fruit bases.

You will find too that many of the wild fruits for which recipes appear in this book also grow in your countries. Because huckleberries are not normally grown here in Britain, I cannot include a recipe for making wines from them, but if you wish to do so you will do very well if you follow the recipe for blackberry wine. If you use sultanas as mentioned in some of my recipes you will have to ask for white raisins.

With best wishes to all my followers in America and Canada – and indeed in all other parts of the world – especially members of the Bravery Wine Club of America.

26
SOME QUESTIONS AND ANSWERS

No matter how many books have been written on wine- and beer-making and no matter how many more will be written there will always be questions that require an answer. This is not because the books available do not try to answer all the questions as they go along. It is simply that problems arise that should not arise, and people who should not have problems do have them. Moreover many people have no problems at all while others seem to have more than their fair share. The fact is that theory and practice are two entirely different things. So let me try to answer a cross-section of the most likely problems to occur.

QUESTION   I have been using your recipes and methods from way back in 1957 when Noel Whitcomb offered his *Daily Mirror* recipe for your Jungle Juice. I was one of the hundred thousand readers who sent for it. Since then I have been most successful in my wine-making, having won many prizes. In your modern methods you recommend a short second period of fermentation in the fermenting pail. Is there any special reason for this?

ANSWER   There is. When you strain the fruit pulp and wring it out as dry as you can, quite a lot of minute particles of fruit pulp are pressed through into the wine. During the secondary short period, where fermentation is less vigorous, many of these solids settle to the bottom of the pail and are left behind when you follow my instructions to 'pour carefully into a gallon jar leaving as much deposit in the pail as you can'. Were it not for this second short period all this rubbish would get into the jar and this would mean further racking later on and perhaps 'off' flavours given into the wine.

QUESTION   Thanks to you, all my wines are first rate. But what puzzles me is that I always get a dryness in the background flavour of my elderberry and sloe wines, even when using 1.6 kg (3½ lb) of sugar per 5 l (5 gall), which I am told is more than I should be using. Can you explain this for me?

ANSWER When using that amount of sugar your wines must be sweet because there is about 450 g (1 lb) of unfermented sugar in every 5 l (1 gall) which, as you say, is too much. The apparent dryness is caused by an excess of tannin which comes from the skins of the elderberries and sloes. When using these in future, ferment the pulp for three days only to prevent too much tannin soaking into the wine. Otherwise, keep the wine for five years – which is rather a long time for anybody to keep wines when they want to drink them. If you ferment the pulp for short periods use not more than 1.350 kg (3 lb) of sugar per 5 l (1 gall).

QUESTION I have some small solids floating just under the shoulders of a gallon jar of brilliantly clear wine and everything I do to get them to settle to the bottom has failed. Can you tell me how to get rid of them?
ANSWER The best way is to insert a funnel and slowly pour in a little similar wine while revolving the jar so that the solids come into the neck. Then add a little more wine to overflow them out. Clean the jar well afterwards and bung it securely.

QUESTION After putting my wines into a jar I find that the yeast is rising up and down inside the jar and I am wondering if it will settle eventually.
ANSWER The problem here is that you have a rather more vigorous ferment than usual for wine in a jar and the upsurge of gas is causing the yeast to rise and fall. As soon as fermentation slows down the amount of gas will diminish, allowing the yeast to settle. So do not let this bother you.

QUESTION I am fairly new to wine-making and fermentation locks. And what bothers me is that for a few weeks after putting the wine into jar and fitting locks the solution bubbles away allowing the gas to escape and all is well. But later on, I find that the solution is not moving, or is on the wrong side. In other words it is drawn up on the in-going side. It would be much appreciated if you would tell me what is wrong.
ANSWER Nothing very much – if anything. It is clear from what you tell me that during the vigorous ferment in the jar all is well. But later when fermentation slows down and the amount of gas being produced is less, so that the pressure under the solution is less, there is a change of temperature which causes the wine to contract or shrink as it becomes cooler. This causes a temporary space in the jar. Since there must be balance between the atmospheric pressures both inside and outside the jar air is drawn in to effect this. Try to keep your wines at a constant temperature and this sort of thing will not occur. But when fermentation has ceased altogether it will be found that the solution in the lock will be drawn up on the in-going side and remain there for a week or two before returning to normal level in the 'U' bend.

QUESTION   In your magazine articles and books you always recommend filling the jar to where the neck begins. I always do this, of course, but later on when a little more space is left in the jar owing to more sugar being fermented out, should I fill up again?

ANSWER   No. You will note that in my recipes I never give the exact amount of water to use, but take into account all the amounts of fruits used. The amount of water used to fill to where the neck begins forms part of the overall amount to use in relation to all the other ingredients. If you keep topping up afterwards you will dilute the flavour and alcohol content so that the yeast will make good the alcohol. If you are making a sweet or medium-sweet wine you will eventually finish up with a dry wine because each dilution of alcohol will induce the yeast to make more until there is no sugar left to be fermented.

QUESTION   I am nearly seventy and deaf, but with my hearing aid I usually manage to understand all that goes on during our wine-making circle's talks. Many of my friends and I have several of your books and we all wonder why you do not give talks to wine-making circles. We are sure that with all your experience you would have much of interest to tell us.

ANSWER   I have been expecting this and since you have asked I will tell you. I used to give talks, travelling all over the place, but being totally deaf myself I found it a bit too much for me. I lost my hearing in 1940 during the war to such an extent that even today I can stand within fifty yards of where giant jet liners take off and not hear a sound. So you are lucky to be able to benefit from a hearing aid. Good luck to you. Incidentally it was owing to being deaf that I took to wine-making to keep myself occupied and then started writing about it.

QUESTION   I have made some marvellous wines from your recipes and methods and have never before had a problem I could not solve myself. But my last batch almost climbed out of the jar to attack me. Masses of froth was climbing up, through the lock and out of the jar and running down the outside of it. Can you tell me what caused this and what I should do if it occurs again?

ANSWER   All that has happened is that, instead of fermentation slowing down as much as expected before the wine was put into the jar, it remained vigorous. When put into the jar the airing probably caused it to become even more vigorous. Thus more froth than usual was produced and this had to escape. If you have this bother again, return the wine to the fermenting vessel, cover as usual and leave a day or two before returning it to the jar.

QUESTION   When corking my wine I like to let the air out of the bottle as the cork goes in. I do this by inserting a piece of string which I pull out as the cork goes in. Even with new string, this always leaves a dirty cloud in the top inch of wine. Can you tell me how to avoid this? A friend of mine gave me this tip.

ANSWER   Yes, and simply by not using string. No harm at all will come – if that is what you are afraid of – of pressing the cork home and compressing the small amount of air between the wine and the cork.

QUESTION   A recently received price list offers Kent Golding hops, Northern Brewer and also Fuggles. Prices varied slightly but this is not what bothers me. With several sorts of hops available, how am I to know which is best to use? And do they vary all that much?

ANSWER   Hops do vary in many ways and, while most recipes recommend a certain variety of hops, it is often a matter of trial and error for many brewers trying to find the hops best suited to the kind of beer they are making. But this would apply only if for some reason the hobbyist feels dissatisfied with the effect in his brews created by the hops he is using.

QUESTION   When opening my bottled beers I usually get a fountain of froth. Sometimes this is so great that I lose a third of a bottle of beer. Yet at other times there is just about the right amount which rises to the top but does not overflow,. and the beer pours well with a good head that remains well.

ANSWER   If you prime at the same rate every time (use the same amount of sugar, that is, for the same amount of beer) it could be that sometimes you prime a day too soon. But it seems more likely to me that your storage area is too easily affected by temperature. Warmth will give rise to excess frothing, though it should not cause fountains of froth. So it would seem that you may be either priming just a bit too soon, or using too much sugar and allowing your beers to become warm. Only you can decide which. It does occur to me that if you use sugar to prime, say, 20 l (4 gall) and have a little less, then this would amount to over-priming. So do make sure how much beer you have before apportioning the priming sugar. And after priming a week in the warm and then a cool place is best.

QUESTION   Having started brewing recently, I have come across the fact that there are top-fermenting and bottom-fermenting yeasts. How do I know which is the best to use?

ANSWER   Top-fermenting beer yeasts are used for all English-type beers but the bottom-fermenting sorts are used mainly in continental beers and for making lager.

QUESTION   I have started using a brewing vessel where the mash comes into contact with the electrical element and find that there is some darkening of my beers. The beers themselves are just as good and I find the vessel excellent for mashing. But my light ales are just that little too dark for a true light ale. This may sound like breaking small stones, but can any harm come to the mash by coming into contact with the electric element?

ANSWER If you mean any harm coming to the beer through metal contact with the mash the answer is no. The darkening you complain of could occur because your mash is rather too stodgy for the vessel (I know which one you are alluding to). Stodgy mashes in this vessel might be subject to slight burning. This does not mean actual burning, but it does cause caramelization of the malt which darkens the beer. A rather dilute mash – that is, not a stodgy one – will prevent this occurring. I would add that this is the only problem – and not a big one – that will occur with this vessel, but as I say, it will not arise if the mash is not too stodgy.

QUESTION Can you tell me whether I obtain more malt from 450 g (1 lb) of malt extract or 450 g (1 lb) of malt?

ANSWER Theoretically, you should be able to obtain from 450 g (1 lb) of malt extract and 450 g (1 lb) of cracked grain malt almost identical quantities of fermentable sugars. But to be able to do this, the sparging of the grain malts (mash) must be perfect (that is, every scrap of fermentable sugars washed of the spent husks).

QUESTION I am making both wines and beers – wines for my wife and beers for myself – and I am puzzled as to how to apportion the yeast I buy for 10 l (2 gall) lots when most packets contain sufficient for 25 or 50 l (5 or 10 gall). Is it of great importance that the 'correct' amount of yeast be used?

ANSWER No, it is not important. A pin-head of yeast will in time produce enough to ferment fifty or even a hundred gallons of wine or beer. But such a small amount would take time to reproduce enough for this. Since it is important to get both wines and beers fermenting vigorously as soon as possible after they are prepared we don't want a waiting period. If I were using a pack of yeast designed for 25 l (5 gall) and I happened to be making 15 or 20 l (3 or 4 gall) of wine or beer, I would lump the lot into the starter solution (sugar and fruit juice in the case of wines, and sugar and malt dissolved in warm water in the case of beers) and get the whole lot fermenting quickly and then use it all. Far better to use too much than too little, and certainly no harm can come of using more than prescribed.

List of Suppliers

There are now suppliers of home wine-making utensils and ingredients in most towns, apart from Boots and other multiple chemists. The list below is of those in larger towns where they cannot be all that far from you, wherever you may live. But there may be one nearer to you that I have not heard about – so ask around.

England

Birmingham Home Brews (Pinnicks), 566-8 Stratford Rd, Sparkhill, Birmingham

Brew-at-Home, 29 Webbs Rd, London SW11

Brewers' Supplies, 97 Dartmouth Rd, Forest Hill, London SE23

Brewing Supplies, 48 Heaviley Rd, Stockport, Cheshire

Busby Ltd, 96 Farringdon Rd, London EC1

Continental Wine Experts, Cawston, Norfolk

Cumbria Home Brews, Brampton, Cumbria

Dermar Home Brew Supplies, 11 Crown St, St Ives, Hunts.

Green, D.F., 135 Lynchford Rd, Farnborough, Hants.

Hidalgo, M. Agusti, 81 Ledbury Rd, London W11

Home Brew Centre, 120 Pinner Rd, Harrow, Middx

Home Brew Specialists, Roundhay Rd, Leeds 8

Home Brewer, The, 19 Desborough Ave, High Wycombe, Bucks.

Home Wine-making Supplies, 17 Portland Rd, Chichester, Sussex

Leigh, Williams, Tattenhall, Chester

Loftus, W.R., 1-3 Charlotte St, London W1 (no mail order)

Loftus, W.R., Rock St, Store, Torquay, Devon (mail order)

Loftus, W.R., 1 Okehampton St, Exeter, Devon

Regency Chateau, 255 Grimsby Rd, Cleethorpes, Lincs.

Rogers (Meads) Ltd, 27 Vicarage Rd, Wednesfield, Staffs.

Semplex, Old Hall Works, Stuart Rd, Higher Tranmere, Birkenhead, Cheshire
Solvino, 678 High Rd, Finchley, London N12
Viking Brews, Clive St, North Shields, Northumberland
Vina Ltd, St Johns Rd, Waterloo, Liverpool 22
Vinopack, 29 Edburton Ave, Brighton, Sussex
Wine World of Huyton, 21 Sherbourne Sq., Huyton, Lancs.
Winecraft, Slate St, Leicester
Wine-Makers Vineyard, 96 Brigstock Rd, Thornton Heath, Surrey

Scotland
The Bachonal, 14 Newton St, Greenock
Glen Brew, 706 Dumbarton Rd (Patrick), Glasgow West

Northern Ireland
Erwin Export Services, (NI)2 17 Shore St, Belfast 15
Ulster Home Brews, 6 Dillons Avenue, Whiteabbey, Co. Antrim

Wales
Home Brew Supplies, 69 Whitechurch Rd, Cardiff

Eire
Quality Home Brews, 79 Braemor Rd, Churchtown, Dublin

USA and Canada
Aetna Bottle Co., 708 Rainier Avenue Sth, Seattle 44, Washington, USA
Wine Supplies, Box 30230-U, Cincinnati O-45230, USA
Bacchanalia 273, H-Riverside Avenue, Westport, Connecticut, USA
Wineart, PO Box 2701, Vancouver 3, BC, Canada (with franchises throughout
Canada and most states in USA)

New Zealand
Brewers Trading Co., PO Box 593, Christchurch (this firm supplies most of the
Australian market)